Festive Holiday Recipes

Also in This Series

Family Favorite Casserole Recipes:
103 Comforting Breakfast Casseroles, Dinner Ideas,
and Desserts Everyone Will Love

No-Bake Desserts:
103 Easy Recipes for No-Bake Cookies, Bars, and Treats

Everyday Dinner Ideas:
103 Easy Recipes with Chicken, Pasta, and Other Dishes Everyone Will Love

Easy Cookie Recipes:
103 Best Recipes for Chocolate Chip Cookies, Cake Mix Creations,
Bars, and Holiday Treats Everyone Will Love

Retro Recipes from the '50s and '60s:
103 Vintage Appetizers, Dinners, and Drinks Everyone Will Love

Essential Slow Cooker Recipes:
103 Fuss-Free Slow Cooker Meals Everyone Will Love

Easy Chicken Recipes:
103 Inventive Soups, Salads, Casseroles, and Dinners Everyone Will Love

Homemade Soup Recipes:
103 Easy Recipes for Soups, Stews, Chilis, and Chowders Everyone Will Love

The Lighten Up Cookbook:
103 Easy, Slimmed-Down Favorites for Breakfast, Lunch, and
Dinner Everyone Will Love

Cake!
103 Decadent Recipes for Poke Cakes, Dump Cakes, Everyday Cakes,
and Special Occasion Cakes Everyone Will Love

Festive Holiday Recipes

103 *Must-Make Dishes for Thanksgiving, Christmas, and New Year's Eve Everyone Will Love*

Addie Gundry

St. Martin's Griffin ⚞ New York

FESTIVE HOLIDAY RECIPES. Copyright © 2018 by Prime Publishing, LLC. All rights reserved. Printed in the United States of America. For information, address St. Martin's Press, 175 Fifth Avenue, New York, N.Y. 10010.

www.stmartins.com

Text and photography © 2018 Prime Publishing, LLC
Photography by Megan Von Schönhoff and Tom Krawczyk

The Library of Congress Cataloging-in-Publication Data is available upon request.

ISBN 978-1-250-14636-6 (trade paperback)
ISBN 978-1-250-14635-9 (ebook)

Our books may be purchased in bulk for promotional, educational, or business use. Please contact your local bookseller or the Macmillan Corporate and Premium Sales Department at (800) 221-7945, extension 5442, or by email at MacmillanSpecialMarkets@macmillan.com.

First Edition: October 2018

10 9 8 7 6 5 4 3 2 1

To the Gundrys—all of you.
Thank you for creating a family for me to spend
every holiday with, filled with love, laughter,
and a whole lot of food and drink.

Contents

3
Main Courses

4
Sides

5
Desserts

6
Drinks

Festive Holiday Recipes

Introduction

Holidays have the potential to be spectacular, memorable, and full of magic. Of course, plenty can go wrong. But putting aside delayed flights, family fights, or burnt turkeys, I believe that the word "holiday" means something remarkable. There's a reason that the familiar song calls it "the most wonderful time of the year." And that phrase does not pertain to a particular day: any holiday, any celebration, and any spirited festivities during this time are what make it enchanting.

So when does this wonderful time begin? For me, it starts early. Yes, I'm one of those buy-pumpkins-in-September, listen-to-Christmas-music-on-Thanksgiving kind of people. The minute the air turns slightly cooler, the leaves look like they may fall, and the smell of cinnamon hits my nose, I am in the spirit. Growing up, my holidays were always anchored in the food my family served. Thanksgiving meant The Best Roast Turkey (page 79) with a side of Green Bean Casserole (page 112), Christmas called for Slow Cooker Cranberry-Mustard Spiral Ham (page 87), and we were constantly baking Lemon Crinkle Cookies (page 193) to bring to friends and family. What I loved most about Thanksgiving were the leftovers, like Traditional Thanksgiving Stuffing (page 100), which we enjoyed the whole weekend following the big day. And it was nearly impossible to sleep the night we hung our stockings by the fire, because our bellies were full and we were hoping to wake up on Christmas day to candy, like Homemade Holiday Reindeer Poop (page 178), delivered by the jolly old man in red.

Although these moments were magical when I was a child, I have found that some of my favorite memories of Thanksgiving, Christmas, and New Year's Eve are as an adult. I remember the first turkey I ever made for my husband, the first Christmas gifts we exchanged, and our first kiss when the ball dropped. I remember enjoying cake and pie at my first work holiday party and having my first "Friends-giving" away from home in France. The reason it is the most wonderful time of the year is because as you grow older, the memories you make grow stronger. The glitter in Santa's eyes never loses its shimmer, and fighting for the wishbone still doesn't feel childish or trivial. As I get older, I've come to understand the magic that the word "holiday" brings.

Why 103 recipes in this holiday cookbook? One hundred recipes felt too rigid—when we open our hearts and our homes to those we love, there is always room for more. When you come to my house, particularly around the holidays, I want you to know you can always bring a friend or two or three. I hope that this book, filled with recipes for the entire season, will bring a little extra holiday cheer into your home.

—Addie Gundry

1

Brunch

Brunch during the holiday season is such an enchanting time. You're still a little sleepy and wrapped up in your pajamas. It's a peaceful bubble of quiet before it's time to load up the car and head over to meet up with the rest of the family. From Wake-Me-Up Cinnamon Rolls (page 9) to Grab 'n' Go Omelet Cups (page 17), there's a brunch recipe here for every family.

Overnight Cinnamon Bread

Yield: Serves 8 to 12 | Prep Time: 20 minutes, plus 8 hours chill time | Cook Time: 35 to 40 minutes

Cinnamon bread was saved for special occasions when I was growing up, and Christmas morning certainly qualifies. You can do all the prep work on Christmas Eve, so you just need to wake up, pop the loaf pans in the oven, and get ready to dig in!

INGREDIENTS

2 cups all-purpose flour, plus extra for the pans

1 cup whole milk

12 tablespoons unsalted butter, melted

¾ cup granulated sugar

½ cup packed light brown sugar

2 large eggs

2 teaspoons ground cinnamon

1 teaspoon baking powder

1 teaspoon baking soda

½ teaspoon salt

DIRECTIONS

1. Coat three 5¾ × 3-inch loaf pans with cooking spray, then sprinkle with flour.

2. Combine all the ingredients in a large bowl and beat until well combined. Pour into the loaf pans, then cover and chill for at least 8 hours, or overnight.

3. Preheat the oven to 350°F.

4. Bake for 35 to 40 minutes, or until a toothpick inserted in the center comes out clean.

5. Slice and serve warm, or let cool completely and wrap individually to give away to guests.

NOTES

If you prefer, you can pour the batter into one 9 × 13-inch baking dish and bake it for 45 to 50 minutes.

Denver Omelet Bake

Yield: Serves 6 to 8 | Prep Time: 15 minutes | Cook Time: 40 minutes

A Denver omelet, also known as a Southwest omelet, is particularly popular in diners in the western part of the United States. Whenever I visit my husband's family in Arizona, I look forward to going out to brunch because the local diner has a Denver omelet that's oh-so-incredible. During holidays when we don't make it out west, I love making this for my husband to remind him of his family back home.

INGREDIENTS

10 large eggs

½ cup cubed ham

⅓ cup chopped red bell pepper

⅓ cup chopped green bell pepper

¼ cup chopped onion

1 teaspoon salt

¼ teaspoon freshly ground black pepper

1 cup shredded cheddar cheese

1 (17.3-ounce) package refrigerated biscuits

DIRECTIONS

1. Preheat the oven to 375°F. Coat a 9 × 13-inch baking dish with cooking spray.

2. In a large bowl, beat the eggs well. Add the cubed ham, red bell pepper, green bell pepper, onion, salt, and pepper and mix well. Stir in the cheese. Cut each biscuit into 6 pieces and stir into the mixture to coat. Pour the batter into the baking dish.

3. Bake for 40 minutes, or until the egg mixture is set and the top is golden brown. Let cool for just 5 minutes before serving.

Wake-Me-Up Cinnamon Rolls

Yield: Makes 9 cinnamon rolls | Prep Time: 50 minutes | Cook Time: 30 minutes

Cinnamon rolls on Christmas morning is one of my favorite Gundry traditions. The filling and the glaze contain a hint of espresso, which helps you tackle the long day ahead.

INGREDIENTS

Rolls

½ cup warm water (120°F)

2¼ teaspoons quick-rise yeast

2½ tablespoons granulated sugar

2¾ cups all-purpose flour, plus extra for the work surface

1 teaspoon salt

¼ cup whole milk

2 tablespoons unsalted butter

1 large egg

Filling

4 tablespoons unsalted butter, cut into small chunks

¼ cup granulated sugar

1 tablespoon ground cinnamon

1 tablespoon espresso powder

Glaze

1 cup powdered sugar, sifted

2 tablespoons whole milk

1 teaspoon espresso powder

½ teaspoon vanilla extract

DIRECTIONS

1. *For the rolls*: Line a 9 × 9-inch baking pan with parchment paper and lightly coat with cooking spray.

2. In a small bowl, combine the warm water, yeast, and 1 teaspoon sugar.

3. Using a stand mixer fitted with the paddle attachment, mix the flour, salt, and remaining sugar briefly to combine.

4. In a small microwave-safe bowl, combine the milk and butter and microwave for 30 seconds. With the mixer on low, add the milk mixture and the egg. Add the yeast mixture. Switch to the dough hook and knead on low for 4 minutes, until smooth.

5. *For the filling*: Preheat the oven to 200°F. In a small microwave-safe bowl, combine the butter, sugar, cinnamon, and espresso powder and microwave for 20 seconds on high, then stir into a smooth paste.

6. Scrape the dough onto a lightly floured surface and use a rolling pin to make a 9 × 15-inch rectangle. Spread evenly with the filling. Roll tightly from the narrow end into a log; cut into nine slices.

7. Fit the 9 rolls into the baking dish. Cover tightly with plastic wrap, turn off the oven, and set the rolls in the warm oven for 20 minutes to rise.

8. Remove the baking dish and remove the plastic wrap. Turn the oven on to 375°F and immediately place the rolls in the oven. Bake for about 30 minutes, or until lightly golden brown. Let cool.

9. *For the glaze*: While the rolls are cooling, stir the powdered sugar, milk, espresso powder, and vanilla in a small bowl until completely smooth. Drizzle over the rolls and serve.

Overnight Cream Cheese French Toast

Yield: Serves 12 | Prep Time: 20 minutes, plus overnight chill time | Cook Time: 45 to 55 minutes

The secret to this recipe is the challah bread. Sweeter than a regular loaf of bread, it pairs even better with the cream cheese and streusel topping.

INGREDIENTS

French Toast

1 (12- to 14-ounce) loaf challah

1 (8-ounce) package cream cheese, room temperature

2 tablespoons powdered sugar

1 tablespoon vanilla extract

8 large eggs

2¼ cups whole milk

⅔ cup packed light brown sugar

¾ teaspoon ground cinnamon

Streusel Topping

⅓ cup packed light brown sugar

⅓ cup all-purpose flour

½ teaspoon ground cinnamon

6 tablespoons unsalted butter, cold, cut into cubes

DIRECTIONS

1. *For the French toast:* Coat a 9 × 13-inch baking dish with cooking spray. Slice the bread, then cut into 1-inch cubes. Spread half of the cubes into the baking dish. Using a hand mixer or a stand mixer fitted with the whisk attachment, beat the cream cheese on medium-high speed until completely smooth. Beat in the powdered sugar and ¼ teaspoon vanilla until combined. Drop spoonfuls of the cream cheese mixture evenly on top of the bread. Layer the remaining bread cubes on top of the cream cheese.

2. Whisk the eggs, milk, brown sugar, cinnamon, and remaining vanilla together until no brown sugar lumps remain. Pour over the bread. Cover the pan tightly with plastic wrap and refrigerate overnight.

3. Preheat the oven to 350°F. Remove the pan from the refrigerator.

4. *For the streusel topping:* In a medium bowl, whisk together the brown sugar, flour, and cinnamon. Cut in the butter cubes with a pastry blender or 2 forks. Sprinkle the topping over the soaked bread.

5. Bake for 45 to 55 minutes, or until golden brown on top. (Bake it for less time if you prefer it to be softer.) Serve immediately. Cover the leftovers tightly and store in the refrigerator for up to 3 days.

NOTES

The topping can be prepared in advance, covered tightly, and stored in the refrigerator overnight. Sprinkle over the soaked bread before baking. For freezing, prepare the recipe through step 4 and freeze for up to two months. Thaw overnight in the refrigerator, then bake as directed.

Granny's Monkey Bread

Yield: Serves 8 | Prep Time: 15 minutes | Cook Time: 30 minutes

I would recommend waiting to serve this until after the Christmas presents have been opened because it's a glorious, sticky, gooey, delicious mess of a dish. (Having extra napkins on hand doesn't hurt either!) It's the perfect pick-me-up, and it pairs equally well with coffee or champagne.

INGREDIENTS

1 cup (2 sticks) unsalted butter, plus extra for the pan

3 (8-ounce) cans refrigerated buttermilk biscuits

1 cup granulated sugar

2 teaspoons ground cinnamon

½ cup packed light brown sugar

DIRECTIONS

1. Preheat the oven to 350°F. Generously coat a Bundt pan with butter.

2. Cut each biscuit into 4 equal pieces. In a bowl or plastic bag, combine the granulated sugar and cinnamon. Drop and roll the pieces of dough in the cinnamon sugar and gently arrange them into the Bundt pan, messily layering them on top of one another.

3. In a small saucepan, combine ½ cup of the remaining cinnamon sugar with the butter and brown sugar. (Discard any remaining cinnamon sugar.) Bring the mixture just to a boil and then immediately remove from the heat. Carefully drizzle the mixture over the rolled dough balls in the pan. Bake for 30 minutes, until golden brown and bubbling.

4. Let rest for about 5 minutes, then cover the pan with a large plate and invert the bread onto the plate. To eat, pull the desired amount off with your fingers and enjoy.

Snickerdoodle Muffins

Yield: Makes 12 muffins │ Prep Time: 15 minutes │ Cook Time: 20 to 25 minutes

Who says the cinnamon-sugar combo needs to be reserved for dessert? This sweet combination is welcome anytime. Each moist, delicious bite is totally worth it; plus, the muffins themselves are oh-so-fluffy.

INGREDIENTS

Muffins

½ cup whole milk

½ teaspoon white vinegar (see note)

1½ cups all-purpose flour

1 teaspoon baking powder

¾ teaspoon cream of tartar

½ teaspoon baking soda

½ teaspoon ground cinnamon

¼ teaspoon salt

¼ teaspoon grated nutmeg

6 tablespoons unsalted butter, softened

½ cup sugar

1 large egg

1 teaspoon vanilla extract

Topping

½ cup sugar

1 tablespoon ground cinnamon

¼ teaspoon grated nutmeg

DIRECTIONS

1. *For the muffins:* Preheat the oven to 350°F. Line a standard-size muffin pan with paper liners (see notes).

2. Combine the milk and vinegar and set aside.

3. In a medium bowl, combine the flour, baking powder, cream of tartar, baking soda, cinnamon, salt, and nutmeg.

4. Using a hand mixer or a stand mixer fitted with the paddle attachment, beat the butter and sugar for 2 minutes, until the mixture is creamy. Scrape down the sides of the bowl. Add the egg and vanilla, then slowly add the flour mixture and the milk mixture, alternating between the two. Beat only until well combined.

5. *For the topping:* In a small bowl, combine the sugar, cinnamon, and nutmeg. Using a ¼-cup measuring cup or a #16 ice cream scoop, dip portions of the batter one at a time into the topping mixture. Use 2 spoons to roll the batter around until well coated, then carefully place the ball in an empty muffin cup. Repeat with the remaining batter.

6. Bake for 20 to 25 minutes, until a toothpick inserted into the center of a muffin comes out clean.

7. Let cool on a wire rack, then serve.

NOTES

The sugar coating on the batter will cause the muffins to stick in the muffin cups if paper liners are not used, so make sure to use them!

You may substitute ½ cup buttermilk for the milk-vinegar mixture if desired.

Grab 'n' Go Omelet Cups

Yield: Makes 24 mini omelets | Prep Time: 10 minutes | Cook Time: 12 to 15 minutes

If you have family staying over, you need a divide-and-conquer plan of attack when it comes to brunch. Smaller, plentiful, varied options allow guests to graze whenever they wake up and drift downstairs, and that's exactly what these bite-size omelets provide. Morning, noon, or night, these little protein-packed egg cups are a great snack.

INGREDIENTS

8 large eggs

2 tablespoons unsalted butter, melted

2 tablespoons heavy cream

Salt and freshly ground black pepper

5 thick slices bacon, cooked and crumbled

½ cup shredded cheddar cheese

3 scallions, chopped

DIRECTIONS

1. Preheat the oven to 375°F. Generously coat a 24-cup mini muffin tin with cooking spray.

2. In a large bowl, beat the eggs, melted butter, and cream until blended and season with salt and pepper. Evenly pour the mixture into muffin cups; each should be about three-quarters full. Sprinkle each with crumbled bacon, cheese, and scallions.

3. Bake for 12 to 15 minutes, or until the eggs are cooked through. Let cool for 5 minutes. Carefully turn the muffin tin over and remove the omelets. Serve.

2

Appetizers

Cooking during the holiday season can be so hectic between figuring out what's going on with the main course, the many must-have sides, and the dessert that the appetizers can often get overlooked. It's always a good idea to have a couple of appetizers handy for people to munch on as they socialize. I'll serve everything from gooey Cheesy Bacon Crescent Bites (page 50) to buzzworthy Vegetarian Spring Rolls (page 69).

Smoked Salmon and Cream Cheese Bites

Yield: Makes 40 bites | Prep Time: 20 to 25 minutes | Cook Time: n/a

If it's your first time hosting Thanksgiving, you can be sure to start on the right foot by putting out these fancy-pants salmon bites. The cucumbers keep these appetizers light and elegant, so your guests won't get too full before dinner.

INGREDIENTS

3 English cucumbers, peeled and cut into ½ inch thick slices

1 (8-ounce) package cream cheese, room temperature

¼ cup crème fraîche (see note)

3 tablespoons chopped fresh dill, plus dill fronds for garnish

1 tablespoon prepared horseradish

1 teaspoon grated lemon zest plus ½ teaspoon lemon juice

¼ cup capers, drained

1 pound smoked salmon, cut into bite-size pieces

DIRECTIONS

1. Using a melon baller, scoop a small depression in the top of each cucumber slice, forming a little cup. Place the cucumber slices on a paper towel upside-down to drain while preparing the cream cheese mixture.

2. In a medium bowl, whisk together the cream cheese, crème fraîche, chopped dill, horseradish, and lemon zest and juice.

3. Scoop 1 teaspoon of the cream cheese mixture into the top of each cucumber slice. Sprinkle a few capers on top of the cream cheese. Add a piece of smoked salmon and top with a dill frond. Arrange on a platter and serve.

NOTES

If you can't find crème fraîche, feel free to substitute sour cream.

Spinach Pie

Yield: Serves 12 | Prep Time: 30 minutes | Cook Time: 1 hour

The creamy, cheesy filling in this appetizer combined with the flaky, buttery phyllo crust will tempt you to head back for seconds. I especially love the surprising hint of nutmeg, which gives the dish a slightly more complex flavor.

INGREDIENTS

4 tablespoons unsalted butter, melted, plus extra for buttering the dish

2 tablespoons olive oil

3 pounds fresh spinach, washed, dried, and coarsely chopped

10 small scallions, finely chopped

2 cups ricotta cheese

8 ounces feta cheese, crumbled

1 cup grated Parmesan cheese

2 large eggs

3 tablespoons finely chopped fresh dill

3 tablespoons finely chopped fresh parsley

¼ teaspoon ground nutmeg

¼ teaspoon kosher salt

¼ teaspoon freshly ground black pepper

6 sheets phyllo pastry (about 17 × 13 inches), defrosted and trimmed to fit

DIRECTIONS

1. Preheat the oven to 350°F. Butter a 9 × 13-inch baking dish.

2. In a large skillet, heat 1 tablespoon of the oil over medium-high heat and add the spinach in handfuls, adding more as the spinach starts to wilt. Cook until all of the spinach is wilted and bright green, about 3 minutes. Transfer the spinach to a colander and drain any excess liquid.

3. Wipe the skillet clean, add the remaining 1 tablespoon oil and then add the scallions. Cook until soft, about 3 minutes. Add the spinach to the skillet with the scallions and cook for an additional 1 to 2 minutes. Transfer to a large bowl and add the ricotta cheese, feta cheese, Parmesan cheese, eggs, dill, parsley, nutmeg, salt, and pepper.

4. Spread half of the filling into the baking dish. Cover with 2 pieces of the phyllo pastry. Brush lightly with melted butter. Top with 1 piece of phyllo. Spread the remaining filling over the phyllo. Top with 2 more pieces of phyllo and brush with melted butter. Top with remaining piece of phyllo and brush with melted butter. Using a sharp knife, mark 12 squares, or more if a smaller portion is desired, by cutting through the top layers of the pastry.

5. Bake for 45 to 55 minutes, until the phyllo pastry is golden, and the filling is bubbling. Use a sharp knife to cut through the squares. Arrange on a platter and serve.

Caramelized Onion Tartlets

Yield: Makes 12 tartlets | Prep Time: 15 minutes | Cook Time: 45 to 52 minutes

These bite-size onion tartlets are ideal for eating on the move. You can grab a couple to snack on as you mingle, keeping your other hand free for a holiday cocktail.

INGREDIENTS

2 tablespoons olive oil

2 cups very thinly sliced yellow onions

1½ tablespoons unsalted butter

½ teaspoon sugar

¼ teaspoon kosher salt

⅛ teaspoon freshly ground black pepper

1 teaspoon balsamic vinegar

Pie dough for 1 single-crust 9-inch pie (store-bought or homemade)

3 to 4 tablespoons crème fraîche (see note)

Fresh thyme sprigs for garnish

DIRECTIONS

1. Preheat the oven to 375°F. Lightly coat a 12-cup mini muffin tin with cooking spray.

2. In a large skillet, heat the oil over low heat. Add the onions, butter, sugar, 1 tablespoon water, salt and pepper and cook for 10 minutes. Add the vinegar and cook for an additional 25 to 30 minutes, until the onions are deep golden brown.

3. While the onions are cooking, roll the pie dough out into a large circle, slightly less than ⅛ inch thick. Cut out 12 rounds using a 3-inch round cookie cutter. Lightly press 1 round into each mini muffin cup. Bake for 10 to 12 minutes, until golden.

4. Remove the shells from the muffin tin and arrange on a platter. Divide the crème fraîche among the shells, top with the caramelized onions, and sprinkle the top with fresh thyme sprigs. Serve.

NOTES

If you can't find crème fraîche, feel free to substitute sour cream.

Baked Zucchini Bites

Yield: Makes 24 bites | Prep Time: 20 minutes | Cook Time: 15 to 17 minutes

Lemon aioli sauce is often paired with crab cakes, but in this case, I've paired it with baked zucchini bites for a produce-centric appetizer. This is a nice one to serve if you have any vegetarians coming over for Thanksgiving and you want to make sure they're eating something memorable.

INGREDIENTS

Zucchini Bites

2 cups shredded zucchini

¾ teaspoon kosher salt

2 large eggs

½ cup diced onion

¼ cup shredded cheddar cheese

¼ cup grated Parmesan cheese

½ cup panko bread crumbs

2 garlic cloves, minced

½ teaspoon dried herbes de Provence

¼ teaspoon freshly ground black pepper

2 chopped scallions for serving

Lemon Aioli

⅓ cup mayonnaise

1 garlic clove, finely minced

½ teaspoon grated lemon zest plus ½ teaspoon lemon juice

Kosher salt and freshly ground black pepper

DIRECTIONS

1. *For the zucchini bites:* Preheat the oven to 400°F. Lightly coat a 24-cup mini muffin tin with cooking spray.

2. Put the shredded zucchini in a medium bowl and sprinkle ¼ teaspoon salt on top. Let sit for 5 minutes, then place the zucchini in a clean tea towel and wring out the liquid.

3. In a large bowl, mix the zucchini, eggs, onion, cheddar cheese, Parmesan cheese, panko, garlic, herbes de Provence, pepper, and the remaining ½ teaspoon salt until well combined. Scoop the mixture into the muffin cups, filling evenly to the top of each one.

4. Bake for 15 to 17 minutes, until golden brown. Let cool in the muffin tin for a few minutes, then transfer to a wire rack.

5. *For the lemon aioli:* In a small bowl, mix the mayonnaise, garlic, and the lemon zest and juice until combined and season with salt and pepper. Sprinkle the scallions over the zucchini bites and serve warm with the aioli.

Slow Cooker Beer Cheese Dip

Yield: Makes 5 cups | Prep Time: 5 minutes | Cook Time: 2 hours

I don't think I've ever had a Thanksgiving dinner where football wasn't playing in the background, and to this day I am quite certain my husband's favorite part of the day is the game and a beer on the couch. It's become as much a part of my holiday tradition as turkey, which is why a football-friendly dip like this is a must-have. As a bonus, by using the slow cooker, I can keep the oven free for dinner!

INGREDIENTS

4 cups shredded triple cheddar cheese (white, sharp, and mild)

1 (8-ounce) package cream cheese

1 cup Guinness or other similar dark ale

1 tablespoon stone-ground mustard

2 scallions, chopped

4 slices bacon, cooked and crumbled

Hot sauce (optional)

Kettle chips and/or pretzel bites for dipping

DIRECTIONS

1. Lightly coat a 6-quart slow cooker insert with cooking spray. Add the cheddar cheese, cream cheese, Guinness, and mustard. Cover and cook for 2 hours on low, stirring occasionally. Transfer to a bowl.

2. Garnish with scallions and bacon, and sprinkle with hot sauce, if desired. Serve with kettle chips and/or pretzel bites.

Crispy Hasselback Potato Bites

Yield: Serves 5 | Prep Time: 15 minutes | Cook Time: 35 to 40 minutes

Another football favorite, these potato bites allow your guests to customize their snacking experience. I like setting up a little snack bar for everyone to load up with whatever they want, which means less work for me. These can be eaten by hand or with a knife and fork.

INGREDIENTS

1 pound small Yukon Gold potatoes, unpeeled, scrubbed

Garlic olive oil

Kosher salt

2 tablespoons grated Parmesan cheese

3 scallions, sliced

DIRECTIONS

1. Preheat the oven to 400°F. Line a baking sheet with aluminum foil.

2. Using a sharp knife, make several cuts through each potato, being careful not to cut all the way through. Place the potatoes on the baking sheet. Rub with the oil and sprinkle with salt. Bake for 30 minutes, or until tender.

3. Sprinkle with the Parmesan cheese.

4. Return to the oven and bake for an additional 5 to 10 minutes, until the cheese has melted.

5. Let cool for 10 minutes, then top with scallions and serve.

Cheesy Popovers

Yield: Makes 6 large or 12 small popovers | Prep Time: 10 minutes | Cook Time: 35 minutes

Similar to England's Yorkshire pudding, this cheesy bread can serve double duty as a snack before Thanksgiving dinner or arranged in a wicker basket to serve alongside the mashed potatoes and turkey! My favorite restaurant in our neighborhood, The Deerpath Inn, serves cheesy popovers around the holidays. I love making them at home and bringing that special night-out feeling to our kitchen.

INGREDIENTS

3 large eggs, room temperature

1 tablespoon unsalted butter, melted and cooled, plus extra for the pan

1 cup all-purpose flour

1 cup whole milk, room temperature

½ teaspoon kosher salt

¾ cup grated cheddar cheese

¼ cup finely minced chives

4 slices bacon, cooked and crumbled

DIRECTIONS

1. Preheat the oven to 450°F.

2. In a medium bowl, whisk the eggs and cooled melted butter. Add the flour, milk, and salt and whisk just until blended. Gently fold in the cheese, chives, and bacon. Do not overmix.

3. Place the popover pan in the oven for 2 to 3 minutes. Remove and grease the popover cups with melted butter.

4. Fill the popover cups two-thirds full with the batter. Bake for 15 minutes. Lower the oven to 350°F and bake for an additional 20 minutes, until the popovers are golden brown and crusty. Do not open the oven door while the popovers are baking!

5. Remove from the oven and make a small slit in the side of each popover with a sharp knife to prevent sogginess. Serve.

NOTES

Do not substitute a muffin pan for the popover pan in this recipe.

Hot Spinach and Artichoke Dip

Yield: Serves 12 | Prep Time: 15 minutes | Cook Time: 40 to 45 minutes

Dips are one of the easiest ways to satisfy your guests during the holidays. This restaurant-quality spinach and artichoke dip is eminently dippable. I suggest serving it with pita chips, but you can offer a few other options too, including tortilla chips and crackers.

INGREDIENTS

1 pound fresh spinach, washed and coarsely chopped

1 (14-ounce) can artichoke hearts, drained and coarsely chopped

1 (8-ounce) package cream cheese, room temperature

1½ cups shredded mozzarella cheese

½ cup shredded Parmesan cheese

½ cup crème fraîche

¼ cup sour cream

1 teaspoon garlic powder

½ teaspoon salt

½ teaspoon freshly ground black pepper

¼ teaspoon ground nutmeg

¼ teaspoon red pepper flakes

Pita chips, for serving

DIRECTIONS

1. Preheat the oven to 350°F. Lightly coat a 9 × 13-inch baking dish with cooking spray.

2. In a large skillet, sauté the spinach until wilted over medium heat. Add the artichoke hearts and cook until any liquid has evaporated, about 3 minutes.

3. Using a hand mixer or a stand mixer fitted with the paddle attachment, beat the cream cheese, mozzarella, Parmesan, crème fraîche, sour cream, garlic powder, salt, pepper, nutmeg, and red pepper flakes on medium speed until smooth. Add the spinach and artichokes and beat until combined. Pour into the baking dish, cover with aluminum foil, and bake for 20 minutes.

4. Remove the foil and bake for an additional 20 to 25 minutes, until bubbling.

5. Serve with pita chips.

NOTES

If you can't find crème fraîche, feel free to substitute additional sour cream.

Holiday Pinwheels

Yield: Makes 64 pinwheels | Prep Time: 30 minutes | Chill Time: 2 hours

Spinach tortillas really come in handy around the holidays since they add a festive green touch to any party spread. You can stick decorative holiday toothpicks in the middle of these pinwheels if you really want to fancy them up.

INGREDIENTS

4 ounces cream cheese, room temperature

4 ounces goat cheese, room temperature

¼ cup raspberry preserves

8 (10-inch) spinach flour tortillas

4 to 5 ounces fresh basil leaves

1 pound thinly sliced deli ham or turkey

DIRECTIONS

1. In a small bowl, combine the cream cheese, goat cheese, and raspberry preserves.

2. Spread the cheese mixture over each of the tortillas; top with the basil leaves and then the slices of ham or turkey.

3. Roll up the filled tortillas jelly roll–style, wrap in plastic wrap or wax paper, and refrigerate for 2 hours. Unwrap and slice diagonally into 1-inch slices. Serve.

Candied Pecans

Yield: Makes 3 cups | Prep Time: 10 minutes | Cook Time: 10 minutes

If you've got guests coming in and out of the house throughout December, it's always nice to have a bowl of candied nuts on a side table for easy munching. Put them in a decorative jar, and you've got a fun gift to give to the neighbors.

INGREDIENTS

1¾ cups granulated sugar

½ cup boiling water

¼ cup packed light brown sugar

1 teaspoon ground cinnamon

¼ teaspoon ground nutmeg

¼ teaspoon cream of tartar

1 pound pecans

1 teaspoon vanilla extract

DIRECTIONS

1. In a medium saucepan, combine the granulated sugar, boiling water, brown sugar, cinnamon, nutmeg, and cream of tartar. Cook over medium heat, stirring until the mixture comes to a boil. Continue to cook at a slow boil for 10 minutes, stirring constantly.

2. Remove from the heat and stir in the pecans, then the vanilla. Stir until the pecans are fully coated.

3. Line a baking sheet with parchment paper and pour the pecans on top. Using a fork, separate the pecans and let cool for 10 to 20 minutes. Pour into a party bowl and serve.

Slow Cooker Crab Dip

Yield: Serves 16 | Prep Time: 15 minutes | Cook Time: 2½ to 3 hours

I like to serve this dip from the slow cooker to keep it fresh and warm. Instead of crackers, feel free to pair it with slices of pita bread or rye bread.

INGREDIENTS

3 (6-ounce) cans lump crab meat, drained and flaked

2 (8-ounce) packages cream cheese, room temperature

1 cup diced red onions

½ cup mayonnaise

½ cup grated Parmesan cheese

4 garlic cloves, minced

4 teaspoons sugar

1 teaspoon grated lemon zest

1 teaspoon Old Bay seasoning

Chopped scallions

Crackers for serving

DIRECTIONS

1. Lightly coat a 6-quart slow cooker insert with cooking spray.

2. Put the crab meat, cream cheese, onions, mayonnaise, Parmesan, garlic, sugar, lemon zest, and Old Bay seasoning in the slow cooker and stir to combine. Cover and cook for 2½ to 3 hours on low, until hot.

3. Garnish with scallions and serve with crackers, keeping the slow cooker on the low or warm setting.

Easy Cheese Dip

Yield: Serves 10 | Prep Time: 10 minutes | Chill Time: 2 hours

This is a fun dish to decorate according to the occasion. If you're at a more sophisticated event, you can garnish with parsley, or if you're entertaining kids, you can add olives and a carrot on top to make a snowman head! Plus, don't forget to grab some crackers to serve it with.

INGREDIENTS

2 (8-ounce) packages cream cheese, room temperature

¼ small onion, finely grated and drained

2 teaspoons Worcestershire sauce

Salt and freshly ground black pepper

1 (10-ounce) jar red pepper jelly

Crackers, for serving

DIRECTIONS

1. In a medium bowl, combine the cream cheese, onion, and Worcestershire sauce and season with salt and pepper. Mix well. Cover the bowl with plastic wrap and refrigerate for 2 hours until firm and the flavors are blended.

2. Remove from the bowl and using your hands, shape into a disk about 2 inches thick on a serving platter. Spoon the red pepper jelly around the outside of the cheese disk and serve with crackers.

Cranberry-Pecan Brie

Yield: Serves 8 | Prep Time: 5 minutes | Cook Time: 25 to 30 minutes

My mother-in-law makes this appetizer every year and it is gone in a flash. Try using the Cranberry Sauce on page 119 for the filling of this gooey and delicious party treat. It's a great way to repurpose elements from your dinner! Serve this Brie with Wasa crackers.

INGREDIENTS

1 (8-ounce) can refrigerated crescent rolls

1 (8-ounce) round Brie cheese

3 tablespoons cranberry sauce

2 tablespoons chopped pecans

1 large egg, beaten

DIRECTIONS

1. Preheat the oven to 350°F. Line a baking sheet with parchment paper and coat lightly with cooking spray. Unroll the crescent roll dough and separate the triangles. Arrange the triangles on the baking sheet in a pinwheel shape with their narrow points touching in the center. Press the points to seal.

2. Slice the Brie in half horizontally and place the bottom half in the center of the dough, cut side up. Spread the cranberry sauce over the top, sprinkle with pecans, and place the remaining half of the Brie on top, cut side down. Bring the outside corner of each crescent dough triangle up over the top of the Brie, pressing the dough firmly to seal. Twist the ends into a pretty design and check to ensure that all seams are sealed around the Brie. Brush with beaten egg.

3. Bake for 25 to 30 minutes, or until golden. Let cool for 5 to 10 minutes. Serve warm.

Penguin Poppers

Yield: Makes 24 penguins | Prep Time: 45 minutes | Chill Time: 5 to 10 minutes

This is a fun appetizer recipe the kids can help you assemble. Just lay out all of the different elements needed for the penguin's body, and it's like a puzzle you get to put together.

INGREDIENTS

1 large carrot, peeled

1 (6-ounce) can small black olives, drained

1 (7.25-ounce) can jumbo black olives, drained

1 (8-ounce) package cream cheese, room temperature

Decorative cocktail picks

1 to 2 cups shredded mozzarella cheese, for decoration

DIRECTIONS

1. Cut the carrot crosswise 6 inches from the thicker end. Cut a small V-shaped notch down the length of the thicker piece of carrot. Slice into ¼-inch-thick disks. These will be the penguins' feet. Cut the smaller end of the carrot into 24 matchsticks to become the beaks of the penguins.

2. Place the matchstick beaks into the hole of the small olives to create penguin heads. To create the body of the penguin, cut a small wedge out of the jumbo olives. Carefully stuff the cavity of the olive with cream cheese. Once all the olives are stuffed, place them in the freezer for 5 to 10 minutes to firm up.

3. To assemble the penguins, slide a head onto the toothpick, followed by the body. Press the tip of the toothpick into one of the feet disks. Display on a bed of shredded mozzarella "snow" and serve immediately.

Italian Sausage–
Stuffed Mushrooms

Yield: Makes 20 mushrooms | Prep Time: 15 minutes | Cook Time: 30 minutes

These sophisticated bites will impress your guests all year round, but especially during the holiday season. I like to use a tiny spoon like a demitasse spoon to scoop in the filling, so I can keep everything as neat as possible and shape the mushrooms exactly as I'd like.

INGREDIENTS

20 (1½-inch) cremini mushrooms

2 tablespoons olive oil

1 cup finely chopped onion

2 tablespoons finely chopped fresh parsley, plus extra for garnish

1 teaspoon fresh thyme leaves or ½ teaspoon dried thyme

8 ounces hot Italian sausage

1 (8-ounce) package cream cheese, room temperature, cut into 1-inch cubes

½ cup finely grated Parmesan cheese

DIRECTIONS

1. Preheat the oven to 350°F. Line a baking sheet with aluminum foil.

2. Wipe the mushrooms with a damp paper towel and remove the stems. Finely mince the stems. Set the caps aside.

3. In a large skillet, heat 1 tablespoon of the oil over medium-high heat. Add the chopped mushroom stems, onion, parsley, and thyme and cook until the vegetables are translucent, about 2 minutes. Add the sausage and cook, using a wooden spoon to stir and break up any clumps, until the sausage has browned, about 4 minutes. Reduce the heat to low and stir in the cream cheese and half of the Parmesan, stirring until the cheese melts—some remaining lumps are fine. Set aside.

4. Place the mushroom caps in a medium bowl and toss with the remaining 1 tablespoon oil to coat. Arrange the caps, open side up, on the prepared baking sheet. Use a teaspoon to spoon the filling into the caps, shaping the tops into mounds. Sprinkle with the remaining Parmesan and bake for about 20 minutes, until the tops are lightly browned and the filling is heated through. Arrange on a platter, garnish with parsley, and serve warm.

Cheesy Bacon Crescent Bites

Yield: Makes 8 rolls | Prep Time: 10 minutes | Cook Time: 15 to 20 minutes

Bacon, crescent rolls, and cheese—I don't know anyone who would turn down that crowd-pleasing combination. It's why I know I can rely on a recipe like this one to be a big hit.

INGREDIENTS

1 (8-ounce) can refrigerated crescent rolls

8 slices bacon, cooked and chopped

4 deli-size slices cheddar cheese, sliced into 4 strips

2 tablespoons olive oil

1 tablespoon sesame seeds

DIRECTIONS

1. Preheat the oven to 350°F. Lightly coat a baking sheet with cooking spray.

2. Separate the dough into 8 triangles. Working with 1 triangle at a time, place 1 tablespoon of chopped bacon in the center. Place 2 strips of cheese on top of the bacon. Roll up, ending at the tip of the triangle, and place on the baking sheet with the tip down.

3. Brush the oil on the crescents and sprinkle with sesame seeds. Bake for 15 to 20 minutes or until golden brown. Cool for 5 minutes and serve.

Cheesy Stuffed Meatballs

Yield: Makes 20 meatballs | Prep Time: 15 minutes | Cook Time: 15 to 20 minutes

Adding cheese to the center of these stuffed meatballs is an unforgettable twist that'll have everyone reaching for seconds. Keep a cup of toothpicks or those fun plastic swords on hand for serving!

INGREDIENTS

1 pound ground turkey

¾ cup panko bread crumbs

½ cup grated Parmesan cheese

½ cup chicken broth

1 large egg

2 tablespoons chopped fresh parsley, plus additional for garnish

2 garlic cloves, minced

1 teaspoon kosher salt

½ teaspoon dried oregano

¼ teaspoon freshly ground black pepper

1 (8-ounce) block mozzarella cheese, cut into twenty ½-inch cubes

1 (24-ounce) jar marinara sauce

DIRECTIONS

1. Preheat the oven to 350°F. Line a baking sheet with aluminum foil, then coat with cooking spray.

2. In a large bowl, combine the turkey, panko, Parmesan cheese, chicken broth, egg, 2 tablespoons parsley, garlic, salt, oregano, and pepper and mix well.

3. Divide the mixture into 20 portions. Form each portion around a cube of mozzarella cheese to make a meatball.

4. Place on the baking sheet and bake for 15 to 20 minutes until fully cooked. While the meatballs cook, heat the marinara sauce. Spoon the marinara sauce over the top of the meatballs and sprinkle with parsley.

Sourdough Pretzels

Yield: Makes 12 pretzels | Prep Time: 1 hour | Cook Time: 15 minutes

I absolutely love soft pretzels, and these homemade pretzels are super fun to make. They will certainly create a buzz at your holiday festivities. I recommend practicing your twisting motion with a piece of string beforehand, so you'll have the technique down pat when you're ready to handle the dough.

INGREDIENTS

3 cups warm water (about 110°F)

2¼ teaspoons active dry yeast

1 teaspoon sugar

1 tablespoon unsalted butter, melted

1 teaspoon salt

3 cups all-purpose flour, plus extra as needed

Olive oil for the bowl

¼ cup baking soda

1 egg yolk, beaten

1 tablespoon coarse salt, poppy seeds, sesame seeds, or caraway seeds

DIRECTIONS

1. Preheat the oven to 450°F. Line a baking sheet with parchment paper.

2. Using a stand mixer fitted with the dough hook, combine 1 cup of the warm water, the yeast, and sugar. Let stand until mixture is foamy, 5 to 10 minutes. Stir in the melted butter and salt. Add the flour, 1 cup at a time, and knead on medium-low speed until a dough forms and is no longer sticky. Add a bit more flour if the dough is too sticky. Continue to knead for 5 minutes, until the dough is smooth and pliable.

3. Transfer the dough to a work surface and form it into a ball. Clean the mixing bowl and coat with oil. Return the dough to the bowl and cover to rest in a warm, dry place for 15 minutes. Meanwhile, in a medium saucepan, boil the remaining 2 cups water with the baking soda.

4. Turn the dough out onto a lightly floured work surface and cut into 12 even pieces. Roll each piece into a rope 15 to 18 inches long. Working with 1 rope at a time, pull the ends up to meet in the middle, twist them a couple of times, and attach them to the bottom edge of the pretzel dough. Place in the baking soda bath for 2 minutes. Carefully remove from the water and place on the baking sheet. Brush the pretzels with the egg yolk and sprinkle with coarse salt.

5. Bake for 10 to 12 minutes, or until golden brown. Serve.

VARIATIONS

Try different toppings, such as poppy seeds, caraway seeds, or a blend of all your favorite spices.

Pretty Party Pinwheels

Yield: Makes 70 pinwheels | Prep Time: 30 minutes | Chill Time: 1 hour

Pinwheels are super easy to throw together for a party. The recipe below gives a vegetarian option for the pinwheel filling, but feel free to change up the ingredients, like adding deli meat or chopped onions, to suit your tastes.

INGREDIENTS

2 (8-ounce) containers garlic and herb cream cheese (such as Kraft), room temperature

4 scallions, finely chopped

1 jalapeño chile, finely chopped

½ teaspoon freshly ground black pepper

10 (10-inch) flour tortillas

5 cups fresh spinach leaves

1 (7.5-ounce) jar sun-dried tomatoes, drained and coarsely chopped

Salsa or hot sauce for serving

DIRECTIONS

1. In a medium bowl, combine the cream cheese, scallions, jalapeño, and pepper. Spread the mixture evenly onto the flour tortillas. Place ½ cup spinach leaves and a few sun-dried tomatoes on each tortilla. Roll up each filled tortilla, like a jelly roll. Place on a platter, cover with plastic wrap, and chill for 1 hour.

2. Using a sharp knife, slice each tortilla roll into ½-inch rounds. Serve with salsa or hot sauce.

Bacon–Brown Sugar Smokies

Yield: Makes about 30 smokies | Prep Time: 30 to 40 minutes, plus 3 hours chill time | Cook Time: 10 to 15 minutes

The combination of salty and sweet makes this New Year's appetizer a grand slam. Make sure to get fancy toothpicks if you want to be extra festive.

INGREDIENTS

Dip

½ cup barbecue sauce

½ cup mayonnaise

¼ cup packed light brown sugar

Smokies

¼ cup barbecue sauce

¼ cup packed light brown sugar

1 pound thick-cut bacon

1 (14-ounce) package all-beef smoked cocktail sausages

Toothpicks

DIRECTIONS

1. *For the dip:* In a small bowl, combine the barbecue sauce, mayonnaise, and brown sugar. Cover and refrigerate for at least 3 hours or overnight.

2. *For the smokies:* Preheat the oven to 425°F. Line a baking sheet with aluminum foil.

3. Place the barbecue sauce in a small, shallow bowl and the sugar in a separate small, shallow bowl. Cut the bacon slices into thirds, widthwise.

4. Roll each smokie in the barbecue sauce and then the brown sugar. Wrap each smokie with a piece of bacon and secure with a toothpick. Place on the baking sheet and bake for 5 to 7 minutes. Flip the smokies and cook for an additional 5 to 7 minutes, or until the bacon is crispy.

5. Serve with the dip.

Sweet Vidalia Onion Dip

Yield: Serves 4 to 6 | Prep Time: 15 minutes | Cook Time: 25 minutes

If there's ever a time to spoil yourself, it has to be the holiday season. The combination of three gooey cheeses makes this a melt-in-your-mouth delight that pairs well with all of your favorite dippable eats, from potato chips to celery sticks to bread slices and more.

INGREDIENTS

1 sweet Vidalia onion

½ red pepper, chopped

1 cup mayonnaise

1 cup sour cream

1 cup shredded white cheddar cheese

½ cup shredded Parmesan cheese

½ cup shredded mozzarella cheese

1 teaspoon Worcestershire sauce

Salt and freshly ground black pepper

Baguette slices and/or bagel chips

DIRECTIONS

1. Preheat the oven to 375°F. Spray an 8 × 8-inch baking dish with cooking spray.

2. Finely slice the onion and soak the slices in cold water for 15 minutes. Drain the onion slices well and pat dry with a clean tea towel.

3. Transfer the onion slices to a large bowl and add the red pepper, mayonnaise, sour cream, cheddar cheese, Parmesan cheese, mozzarella cheese, Worcestershire sauce, salt, and pepper. Stir to combine. Taste and adjust the seasoning if needed.

4. Pour into the prepared baking dish and bake for 25 minutes, until the mixture is bubbling and brown on top. Serve with toasted baguette slices and/or bagel chips.

Loaded Deviled Eggs

Yield: Serves 12 | Prep Time: 20 to 30 minutes | Cook Time: n/a

These deviled eggs add an elegant touch to any sophisticated New Year's Eve party. They're loaded with bacon and chives, giving them a savory kick that elevates them above ordinary deviled eggs.

INGREDIENTS

12 large eggs, hard-boiled, cooled, and cut in half

6 slices bacon, cooked and crumbled, plus additional for garnish

2 tablespoons mayonnaise

2 tablespoons finely grated cheddar cheese

2 teaspoons chopped fresh chives, plus additional for garnish

1 teaspoon apple cider vinegar

1 teaspoon dry mustard

¼ teaspoon garlic powder

¼ teaspoon kosher salt

¼ teaspoon freshly ground black pepper

5 to 6 tablespoons sour cream

Paprika

DIRECTIONS

Remove the egg yolks from the egg halves. Place the yolks in a medium bowl, then add the bacon, mayonnaise, cheese, chives, vinegar, dry mustard, garlic powder, salt, and pepper and stir to combine. Stir in 5 tablespoons sour cream, check the consistency, and add 1 more tablespoon if needed. Scoop the yolk mixture into the egg halves and pile high. Arrange the eggs on a platter, sprinkle with paprika, bacon, and chives, and serve.

Pork Potstickers

Yield: Makes 48 potstickers | Prep Time: 30 minutes | Cook Time: 30 minutes

Crispy, savory, and filling, these Pork Potstickers are everything you want out of an appetizer.

INGREDIENTS

1 pound ground pork

½ cup minced bamboo shoots

¼ cup minced fresh ginger

6 scallions, minced

6 cremini mushrooms, minced

3 tablespoons soy sauce

2 tablespoons sesame oil

2 tablespoons cornstarch

1 tablespoon hoisin sauce

2 teaspoons minced garlic

1 teaspoon Chinese five-spice powder

½ to 1 teaspoon cayenne pepper

48 round dumpling wrappers

¼ cup vegetable oil

Peanut sauce or soy sauce for serving

DIRECTIONS

1. In a large bowl, mix the ground pork, bamboo shoots, ginger, scallions, mushrooms, soy sauce, sesame oil, cornstarch, hoisin sauce, garlic, five-spice powder, and cayenne pepper until combined.

2. Place 1½ teaspoons of the filling in the center of a dumpling wrapper. Wet the edges with water, then fold the circle in half without sealing. Pinch 1 end closed, then create pleats, pressing against the flat side to seal. Flatten the bottom slightly. Repeat with the remaining filling and wrappers.

3. In a large skillet, heat 2 to 3 tablespoons vegetable oil over high heat. Add the potstickers in batches and fry for 2 to 3 minutes, until golden. Add ½ cup water to the skillet, cover, and cook until the water is boiled away, about 3 minutes. Uncover, reduce the heat to medium, and cook for an additional 2 to 3 minutes. Add more vegetable oil, as needed, and repeat until all potstickers are cooked. Serve with sauce.

Deep-Fried Matzo Balls

Yield: Makes 15 matzo balls | Prep Time: 10 minutes | Cook Time: 35 minutes

I try not to indulge in deep frying too much around the holidays, but I just can't resist these matzo balls. Typically, I've only eaten matzo balls in soups before, but when a coworker suggested that I try deep-frying them, I had to give it a go. Make sure to stand far enough away from the stove that you don't get splattered by any hot oil.

INGREDIENTS

½ cup mayonnaise

2 tablespoons red pepper jelly

1 teaspoon lemon juice

1 (2.25-ounce) packet matzo ball mix

1 tablespoon dried chives

Vegetable oil for frying, plus extra as needed for the matzo ball mix

2 large eggs, plus extra as needed for the matzo ball mix

2 cups panko bread crumbs

Salt and freshly ground black pepper

DIRECTIONS

1. In a small bowl, combine the mayonnaise, jelly, and lemon juice. Mix well and then cover with plastic wrap. Refrigerate until ready to serve.

2. Prepare and roll the matzo ball mix according to the package directions, adding chives to the mix. The balls should be rolled to about walnut size. Boil the matzo balls according to the package directions and drain on paper towels.

3. Add oil to a large pot until it measures about 1 inch deep and heat over medium-high heat until around 360°F.

4. Place the eggs in a shallow bowl and whisk. Place the panko in another shallow bowl and season with salt and pepper. Roll each ball in the eggs and then in the panko.

5. Working in batches, add the matzo balls carefully to the hot oil and fry until light golden brown. Drain on paper towels and sprinkle with salt to taste. Let cool slightly and serve with the red pepper dip.

Vegetarian Spring Rolls

Yield: Makes 6 rolls | Prep Time: 45 minutes | Cook Time: 15 minutes

The first time I made my own spring rolls, I put way too much filling in the center, and the wrapper was bursting at the seams. Now I know to start out conservatively and add more filling a bit at a time. I make these for New Year's since they're easy to load onto a plate and take with me as I chat with friends. Serve these rolls with your favorite dipping sauce.

INGREDIENTS

2 teaspoons sesame oil

1 tablespoon finely chopped ginger

1 tablespoon finely chopped garlic

4 scallions, white and green parts separated and finely chopped

1 large carrot, peeled and julienned

1 red bell pepper, julienned

2 cups finely shredded napa cabbage

¼ cup chopped fresh Thai basil or cilantro

2 teaspoons light brown sugar

2 teaspoons soy sauce

1 teaspoon kosher salt

1 teaspoon freshly ground black pepper

6 spring roll wrappers

DIRECTIONS

1. In a large skillet or wok, heat the oil over medium heat. Add the ginger and garlic and cook for 30 seconds. Add the scallion whites and cook for 30 seconds. Add the carrot, red bell pepper, cabbage, Thai basil, and sugar. Cook for 1 minute. Add the soy sauce, salt, and pepper and cook for 2 minutes. Mix in the scallion greens and remove the skillet from the heat. Transfer to a colander over a bowl, drain the liquid, and let the mixture cool.

2. Submerge a spring roll wrapper in water for 15 seconds. Place on a tea towel, then set on a work surface. Place about one-sixth of the filling near the bottom edge of the wrapper, and then fold the bottom of the wrapper up over the filling. Tuck in the right and left sides and continue to roll the wrapper to the top edge. Press gently to seal. Repeat with the remaining rolls and filling. Serve.

Easy Garlic-Parmesan Knots

Yield: Makes 16 knots | Prep Time: 15 minutes | Cook Time: 8 to 10 minutes

Garlic knots take regular old garlic bread to a new level. The twists and turns create new nooks and crannies for the butter mixture to soak into, adding even more flavor to every bite.

INGREDIENTS

4 tablespoons unsalted butter, melted

2 tablespoons grated Parmesan cheese

2 teaspoons minced garlic

½ teaspoon dried herbes de Provence

½ teaspoon dried parsley flakes

¼ teaspoon kosher or sea salt

1 (16-ounce) tube refrigerated buttermilk biscuits

DIRECTIONS

1. Preheat the oven to 400°F. Line a baking sheet with parchment paper and coat with cooking spray. In a small bowl, whisk together the melted butter, cheese, garlic, herbes de Provence, parsley, and salt.

2. Halve each biscuit. Roll each biscuit half into a 5-inch rope, about ½ inch thick, then tie into a knot. Place the knots on the baking sheet. Brush the knots with half of the butter mixture.

3. Bake for 8 to 10 minutes, until golden brown. Brush with the remaining butter mixture and serve hot.

Lime-Tequila Shrimp Kebabs

Yield: Serves 6 to 8 | Prep Time: 15 minutes, plus 2 hours chill time | Cook Time: 5 minutes

Kebabs are ideal for party situations since they're easy to nibble on while you're meandering around the room. The dashes of lime and tequila add an appropriately festive New Year's Eve twist.

INGREDIENTS

¼ cup lime juice, plus
2 limes, cut into wedges

¼ cup tequila

¼ cup olive oil

½ jalapeño chile, minced

1 garlic clove, minced

¼ teaspoon paprika

¼ teaspoon ground cumin

Pinch red pepper flakes

Pinch salt

Pinch freshly ground black pepper

1 pound large shrimp, peeled and deveined

1 red bell pepper, cut into wedges

1 onion, cut into wedges

6 to 8 wooden skewers, soaked in water

Yellow rice for serving

DIRECTIONS

1. In a large bowl, combine the lime juice, tequila, oil, jalapeño, garlic, paprika, cumin, red pepper flakes, salt, and pepper. Add the shrimp to the bowl and toss. Cover and refrigerate for 2 hours.

2. Preheat the grill pan over medium heat. Alternate the shrimp, red bell pepper wedges, onion wedges, and lime wedges on the skewers. Place the skewers on the grill pan and cook for 5 minutes. Remove the food from the skewers, if desired, and serve with yellow rice.

Cream Cheese Wontons

Yield: Makes 12 wontons | Prep Time: 20 minutes | Cook Time: 10 minutes

The cream cheese filling in these wontons contrasts nicely with the crispy exterior, making an appetizer that'll have the whole crowd talking.

INGREDIENTS

½ (8-ounce) package cream cheese, room temperature

1 scallion, minced

1 teaspoon lemon pepper

½ teaspoon garlic powder

½ teaspoon paprika

Pinch sea salt

12 wonton wrappers (see note)

Vegetable or canola oil, for frying

Plum sauce and/or sweet and sour sauce

DIRECTIONS

1. In a small bowl, combine the cream cheese, scallion, lemon pepper, garlic powder, paprika, and sea salt. Using a small ice cream scoop, place a teaspoon-size ball of cream cheese mixture in the center of each wrapper. Dip your finger in water and moisten the corners of the wrapper, then fold up and seal.

2. Heat the oil in a large skillet over medium heat. Add the wontons and fry until golden brown on each side, about 5 minutes. Transfer to a wire rack and let cool slightly. Serve with plum sauce or sweet and sour sauce, or both!

NOTES

If you can't find wonton wrappers, feel free to cut an egg roll wrapper into 4 small squares.

3

Main Courses

If you're tasked with hosting a holiday feast this year, whether Thanksgiving, Christmas, or Hanukkah, you have to make sure the star of the show—the main course—is ready to shine! While cooking an entire turkey or roast may seem overwhelming, these recipes make it easy and delicious.

The Best Roast Turkey

Yield: Serves 10 to 12 | Prep Time: 20 minutes | Cook Time: 3 to 3½ hours

All you need are a few seasonings and some veggies to create a memorable star of the show.

INGREDIENTS

1 (15-pound) whole turkey, fresh or completely thawed if frozen

1 teaspoon salt

½ teaspoon freshly ground black pepper

1 onion, quartered

2 stalks celery, cut into 4-inch pieces

3 sprigs fresh thyme, plus extra, chopped, for serving

3 sprigs fresh sage, plus extra, chopped, for serving

4 tablespoons unsalted butter, softened

1 teaspoon poultry seasoning

Water, chicken broth, or turkey bone broth, as needed

DIRECTIONS

1. Preheat the oven to 400° F. Prepare a large roasting pan with high sides and a baking rack set inside it. Coat the pan and rack with cooking spray.

2. Remove any wire from the turkey, trim excess fat, remove giblets, and then pat it dry inside and out. Use your fingers to pull the skin away from the meat in the breast area. Position the turkey, breast side up, in the roasting pan.

3. Sprinkle the salt and pepper in the cavity, rubbing to cover the surfaces. Tuck the onion, celery, 2 thyme sprigs, and 2 sage sprigs into the cavity. Use kitchen twine, doubled, to tie a bow to keep the legs together.

4. Finely mince the leaves from the remaining thyme and sage sprigs and put them in a small bowl. Add the butter and poultry seasoning and mix to make a paste. Rub 3 tablespoons of the butter underneath the turkey's skin, reserving the rest for later. Add 1 cup water to the roasting pan.

5. Roast the turkey for 1 hour. Brush with the remaining 1 tablespoon butter and lower the oven temperature to 350°F. Continue to roast for 2 to 2½ hours until an instant-read thermometer inserted in the thickest part of the breast registers 170°F. Add additional water or broth as necessary to maintain at least ½ inch of liquid in the pan.

6. Remove from the oven, cover loosely with foil and a doubled large tea towel and let stand for 30 minutes. Transfer the turkey to a carving board. Carve the turkey, garnish with chopped thyme and sage, and serve.

NOTES

See the Stovetop Turkey Gravy recipe on page 83 for instructions on how to use the pan drippings to make gravy.

Slow Cooker Turkey Breast

Yield: Serves 5 to 6 | Prep Time: 5 minutes | Cook Time: 1 hour on high, plus 1½ hours on high or 3½ hours on low

This recipe is a great way to serve a holiday roast turkey when you have a small guest list. Or if your family prefers mostly white meat, this will give you more of that without moving to a larger, unwieldy bird. Don't worry; you'll likely still have extra for sandwiches later—arguably the best thing about Thanksgiving dinner!

INGREDIENTS

1 (5½-pound) bone-in turkey breast

2 tablespoons fresh parsley leaves

1 tablespoon fresh rosemary leaves

1 tablespoon fresh sage leaves, plus extra for garnish

1 teaspoon salt

8 tablespoons unsalted butter, softened

2 tablespoons Worcestershire sauce

DIRECTIONS

1. Coat a 6-quart slow cooker insert with cooking spray. Use an 18-inch length of aluminum foil to roll into a tube and then coil into a figure eight. Place it in the bottom of the slow cooker to allow the turkey to rise above accumulating juices.

2. Trim the turkey breast, remove the pop-up indicator if it has one, and pat dry with paper towels.

3. Use your fingers to separate the skin from the breast meat, creating a pocket between the two.

4. Chop the parsley, rosemary, and sage. Sprinkle the salt over them, continue to chop until minced, then place in a small microwave-safe bowl. Add the softened butter and mash into a paste. Insert half of this mixture into the pocket you have formed, spreading and smoothing into a thin layer over the breast meat. Set the remaining mixture aside.

5. Place the turkey, skin side up, on the foil base in the slow cooker. Cover and cook for 1 hour on high.

6. Add the Worcestershire sauce to the remaining herb mixture and microwave about 30 seconds, until liquified. Stir well and brush over the surface of the turkey. Cover and cook for 1½ hours on high or for 3½ hours on low, until a thermometer inserted in the thickest part of the breast registers between 165°F and 172°F. (The temperature will rise as the turkey rests before slicing.)

7. Remove the turkey, cover loosely with foil, and let rest for 20 minutes before slicing.

8. Reserve the pan juices to make a gravy. (See the gravy recipe on page 83.)

9. Garnish with fresh sage and serve.

NOTES

When shopping, have in mind the size of your slow cooker so that the breast will fit with plenty of room all around. Make sure to also consider the space between the top of the turkey and the lid of the slow cooker.

The turkey may be cooked up to two days before serving. Let it cool completely, cover tightly, and refrigerate. Slice just before using.

NOTES

If cooking The Best Roast Turkey (page 79), mince another 2 tablespoons of the fresh thyme and sage leaves and use to flavor the gravy and as a garnish.

If cooking Slow Cooker Turkey Breast (page 80), halve this recipe and cook it in a small saucepan.

Stovetop Turkey Gravy

Yield: Makes 4 cups | Prep Time: 10 minutes | Cook Time: 10 minutes

This gravy recipe is the perfect companion to The Best Roast Turkey (page 79). It's your chance to be resourceful and create your own gravy recipe from scratch, using ingredients you already have lying around the house. The wine keeps the gravy silky-smooth.

INGREDIENTS

3 cups drippings from turkey roasting pan

Chicken broth or turkey broth, as needed

4 tablespoons unsalted butter

¼ cup all-purpose flour

1 cup white wine

1 tablespoon finely minced fresh sage

Salt and freshly ground black pepper

DIRECTIONS

1. Carefully pour the pan drippings through a sieve into a measuring cup. Drop in 3 or 4 ice cubes, which will solidify the fat and make it easier to remove. Let stand for 5 minutes, then scoop the fat from the juices. If you do not have 3 cups, add broth to reach that amount.

2. In the now-empty but not washed roasting pan (or a medium saucepan), melt the butter over medium-high heat and use a whisk to stir in the flour, stirring and scraping until all of the flour is absorbed by the butter, about 2 minutes. Slowly add the wine, stirring to pick up any browned bits from the pan. Then whisk constantly while slowly adding the remaining wine and the reserved drippings. Continue to cook until the gravy thickens, about 3 minutes, adding extra broth if necessary to thin the gravy to the desired consistency. Just before serving, stir in the sage and season with salt and pepper to taste.

TO MAKE AHEAD

You can make gravy without using drippings. In a medium saucepan, melt 4 tablespoons butter and add ½ cup finely chopped onion and ½ cup finely chopped celery. Add the flour, white wine, and broth as directed, and season as directed with the sage, salt, and pepper. Be sure to use a very flavorful store-bought or homemade broth. If you need to keep the gravy warm before serving, pour it into a thermal container until ready to serve.

Roasted Cornish Hens and Vegetables

Yield: Serves 4 | Prep Time: 30 minutes | Cook Time: 45 to 55 minutes

If you're feeding a small group for Thanksgiving, then it might not make sense to cook a whole turkey. This Cornish hen alternative allows you to enjoy a special Thanksgiving dinner without getting bogged down in a fridge stuffed with leftovers.

INGREDIENTS

4 Cornish game hens, rinsed and patted dry

Salt and freshly ground black pepper

6 garlic cloves, minced

2 tablespoons olive oil

2 tablespoons smoked paprika

2 teaspoons chili powder

¾ cup chicken broth

2 teaspoons kosher salt

16 ounces baby carrots

1 large onion, chopped

½ cup white wine

Chopped fresh parsley

DIRECTIONS

1. Preheat the oven to 425°F.

2. Rub the insides of the Cornish hens with salt, pepper, and half of the garlic.

3. In a large bowl, combine the oil, paprika, chili powder, and the remaining garlic. Add ¼ cup of the chicken broth and stir to combine. Use two-thirds of this mixture to rub all over the outside of the Cornish hens. Season with salt.

4. Toss the carrots and onion in the remaining mixture to coat. Season with salt and pepper. Place the vegetables in a large roasting pan. Place the hens breast-side up on top of the vegetables.

5. Roast the hens for 30 to 35 minutes. Meanwhile, in a medium bowl, combine the wine and the remaining ½ cup chicken stock.

6. Reduce the oven temperature to 350°F. Remove the roasting pan from the oven and pour the wine mixture over the hens and into the bottom of the roasting pan. Return to the oven and roast for an additional 15 to 20 minutes, basting the hens occasionally with the pan juices, until the hens' juices run clear when poked with a knife.

7. Cut the hens in half, if desired, or leave whole. Arrange the hens and the vegetables on a platter, sprinkle with parsley, and serve.

Slow Cooker Cranberry-Mustard Spiral Ham

Yield: Serves 4 | Prep Time: 10 minutes | Cook Time: 4 to 5 hours on low

I love this recipe because it keeps the oven free so I can warm up side-dish casseroles, bake a pie, or bake some rolls throughout the day. The cranberry sauce gives a classic ham recipe a fun holiday twist.

INGREDIENTS

2 (14-ounce) cans jellied or whole-berry cranberry sauce

1 cup packed light brown sugar

½ cup chicken broth

3 tablespoons whole-grain mustard

1 (6-pound) fully cooked bone-in spiral-cut ham

DIRECTIONS

1. In a large saucepan, combine the cranberry sauce, brown sugar, and broth. Bring to a boil over medium-high heat. Reduce the heat to low and simmer, uncovered, for 10 minutes or until slightly thickened. Remove from the heat and whisk in the mustard.

2. Coat a 6-quart slow cooker insert with cooking spray and add the ham. Pour the sauce over the top of the ham and cook for 4 to 5 hours on low, until an instant-read thermometer reaches 140°F and the ham is warmed through.

3. Carve the ham and serve with the sauce.

Olive Oil Roast with Red Wine Jus

Yield: Serves 6 to 8 | Prep Time: 15 minutes | Cook Time: 2 hours

It's not quite Christmas dinner until the savory, juicy roast gets placed dead center on a serving platter. The red wine jus really helps preserve the flavors of the meat, so you get a tender, moist bite every time.

INGREDIENTS

1 (4- to 5-pound) eye of round roast

1 tablespoon olive oil

4 garlic cloves, minced

Kosher salt and freshly ground black pepper

2 sprigs fresh thyme

½ cup dry red wine

½ cup beef broth

2 tablespoons unsalted butter, cold, cut into cubes

DIRECTIONS

1. Remove the roast from the fridge and let the roast sit at room temperature for 1 hour. Preheat the oven to 500°F. Generously coat a roasting pan with cooking spray.

2. In a small bowl, combine the oil, garlic, 2 teaspoons salt, 1 teaspoon pepper, and thyme. Rinse and pat the roast dry, then rub with the garlic mixture. Transfer to the roasting pan and roast for 25 minutes.

3. Reduce the oven temperature to 170°F. Remove the pan from the oven and cover tightly with aluminum foil. Return to the oven and roast for 1 hour, or until an instant-read thermometer insterted in the thickest part of the meat registers 120 to 125°F for rare, 130 to 140°F for medium-rare, or 140 to 150°F for medium. (The USDA recommends a minimum internal temperature of 145°F.)

4. When the roast is finished, remove from the pan and let rest while preparing the jus. Place the roasting pan over medium-high heat on the stove. Add the wine and broth. Bring to a simmer and reduce the liquid by half; lower the heat to medium-low and whisk in the cubes of butter one at a time until they're incorporated. Add salt and pepper to taste.

5. Slice the roast into ½-inch-thick slices and serve with the pan sauce poured on top.

Company-Ready Brisket

Yield: Serves 6 to 8 | Prep Time: 10 minutes | Cook Time: 3 hours

Using an onion soup mix packet really cuts the work in half. You don't need to raid the spice cabinet to see what you can use for seasoning—it's all provided for you!

INGREDIENTS

1 (4½–5-pound) beef brisket

Salt and freshly ground black pepper

1 (15-ounce) can tomato sauce

1 (14.5-ounce) can diced tomatoes

1 (1-ounce) packet onion soup mix

1 large onion, cut into chunks

DIRECTIONS

1. Preheat the oven to 325°F. Coat a 9 × 13-inch baking dish with cooking spray.

2. Place the beef brisket in the baking dish. Season both sides with salt and pepper. In a large bowl, combine the tomato sauce, diced tomatoes, and onion soup mix. Pour over the brisket. Scatter the onion chunks around the dish. Loosely cover the brisket with aluminum foil and cook for 3 hours, or until completely tender (the internal temperature should be above 145°F).

3. Let rest for 10 minutes, then carve the brisket and serve with the pan juices with the fat removed.

Leftover Turkey Shepherd's Pies

Yield: Serves 4 | Prep Time: 10 minutes | Cook Time: 20 to 30 minutes

Think of this as more of a guide than a recipe. Anything you have left over from the holiday meal is perfect for this dish. In addition to leftover turkey, you can use leftover holiday peas (page 140), carrots (page 139), and mashed potatoes (page 99).

INGREDIENTS

1½ cups chopped cooked turkey

1 cup gravy

½ cup cooked peas

½ cup chopped cooked carrots

2 cups mashed potatoes

DIRECTIONS

1. Preheat the oven to 350°F. Lightly coat 4 (8-ounce) ramekins with cooking spray.

2. In a large bowl, combine the turkey, gravy, peas, and carrots. Divide the mixture between the ramekins. Top each with ½ cup mashed potatoes. Do not over-smooth the tops; the peaks will brown for a pretty finish. Bake for 20 to 30 minutes, until bubbling and the tops are golden.

3. Let cool for 10 minutes, then serve.

Christmas Leftovers Panini

Yield: Serves 1 | Prep Time: 10 minutes | Cook Time: 8 to 10 minutes

For the first few days after Christmas, my fridge is packed with all sorts of oddly sized storage containers filled with leftovers. And while it's nice to experience "take two" of Christmas dinner, I love getting the chance to mix things up and reuse my leftovers to make something new and exciting.

INGREDIENTS

2 tablespoons unsalted butter

2 large slices bread (white or whole wheat)

2 slices Swiss cheese

2 tablespoons Dijon mustard

2 tablespoons mayonnaise

½ cup turkey breast or ham

¼ cup cranberry sauce

DIRECTIONS

1. Heat an electric griddle or panini press to medium heat.

2. Spread the butter on 1 side of each slice of bread. Lay 1 slice of the cheese on the unbuttered side of 1 slice of bread. Spread the mustard and mayonnaise over the cheese. Top with the turkey, cranberry sauce, and remaining slice of cheese. Top with remaining slice of bread, butter-side up.

3. Place on the electric griddle or press and cook for 8 to 10 minutes, until the cheese is melted and the bread is toasted. If you don't have an electric griddle or press, feel free to use a ridged grill pan and press a cast-iron skillet on top. Serve.

4

Sides

After everyone's done watching the football game or exchanging presents, it's finally time to get settled in for the evening and enjoy what the holiday season is all about: spending time with friends and family. The best holiday dinners involve chatter, laughter, and of course, plenty of good food to go around (with enough to spare for leftovers!). The main course may be the star of the show, but the side dishes are what really make a holiday meal shine.

Garlic and Chive Mashed Potatoes

Yield: Serves 8 | Prep Time: 20 minutes | Cook Time: 45 to 60 minutes

Growing up, I was in charge of the potato peeling and mashing during Thanksgiving celebrations. I'd set up shop at the kitchen table with my potato peeler and a huge stack of potatoes and peel away as I chatted with my family bustling about in the kitchen. I have fond memories of that time, and I know that these flavorful potatoes are a must at all of my future Thanksgivings.

INGREDIENTS

Roasted Garlic

1 large head garlic

2 tablespoons olive oil

Mashed Potatoes

4 pounds Yukon Gold potatoes, peeled and quartered

Kosher salt

1⅓ cups half-and-half

4 tablespoons unsalted butter, softened

¼ cup sour cream

¼ cup grated Parmesan cheese

1 tablespoon minced fresh chives, plus extra for garnish

¼ teaspoon freshly ground black pepper

DIRECTIONS

1. *For the roasted garlic.* Preheat the oven to 400°F.

2. Cut off the top of the garlic head, exposing the cloves. Drizzle with the oil. Wrap the head of garlic in aluminum foil and roast for 30 to 40 minutes, until a center clove is soft when a paring knife is inserted. Let cool slightly, then squeeze out the cloves. Mash them with a fork and set aside.

3. *For the mashed potatoes:* Put the potatoes and a pinch of salt in a large saucepan and add cold water to cover the potatoes. Bring to a boil and cook for 15 to 20 minutes, until tender.

4. Pour the half-and-half into a small microwave-safe bowl and microwave until warm, about 1 minute, or pour into a saucepan and heat until warm, about 3 minutes.

5. Drain the potatoes and return them to the pot. Mash the potatoes with a potato masher, then beat with a hand mixer until the desired consistency is reached.

6. Add the warmed half-and-half, roasted garlic cloves, butter, sour cream, cheese, chives, 1 teaspoon salt, and pepper and beat until incorporated. Sprinkle with chives and serve.

Traditional Thanksgiving Stuffing

Yield: Serves 6 to 8 | Prep Time: 10 minutes | Cook Time: 2 hours, 20 minutes

To save time on the day of, I always bake and dry out the bread the night before and leave it uncovered on the counter until the morning when I'm ready to make the stuffing. Go easy when you add the chicken broth to make sure your stuffing has the consistency you desire.

INGREDIENTS

1 pound day-old white French bread, diced into 1-inch cubes and dried

1 cup (2 sticks) unsalted butter

1 extra-large Vidalia onion, finely diced (about 2½ cups)

1 red onion, chopped

1½ cups finely chopped celery

2½ cups low-sodium chicken broth

⅔ cup minced fresh flat-leaf parsley, plus additional leaves for garnish

¼ cup minced fresh sage, plus additional leaves for garnish

2 tablespoons minced fresh rosemary

2 tablespoons thyme

Salt and 1 teaspoon freshly ground black pepper

2 large eggs

Minced fresh chives

DIRECTIONS

1. Preheat the oven to 250°F. Lightly coat a rimmed baking sheet with cooking spray. Place the bread cubes on the sheet and bake, stirring occasionally, until dried out, about 45 minutes. (You must begin with very dry bread or it'll turn to mush.) Let cool completely, then transfer to a very large bowl.

2. Increase the oven temperature to 350°F. Coat a 9 × 13-inch baking dish with cooking spray and set aside.

3. In a large skillet, add 12 tablespoons of the butter and heat over medium-high heat to melt.

4. Add the Vidalia onion, red onion, and celery and cook, stirring frequently, until the vegetables have softened and are just beginning to lightly brown, about 10 minutes. Transfer the vegetables to the bowl with the bread. Add 1¼ cups of the broth, the parsley, sage, rosemary, thyme, salt, and pepper and toss well to combine.

5. In a small bowl, whisk the remaining 1¼ cups chicken broth with the eggs. Pour the mixture over the bread and toss well to combine. Turn the mixture out into the prepared baking dish.

6. Dice the remaining 4 tablespoons butter into 8 to 10 pieces and evenly dot the butter over the top of the stuffing. Cover with aluminum foil and bake for 40 minutes. Uncover and bake for an additional 40 to 45 minutes, or until the top is a light golden brown. Sprinkle with chives, and parsley and sage leaves, and serve immediately.

The stuffing is best warm and fresh
but will keep airtight in the
fridge for up to 5 days.
Reheat gently
as desired.

Fall Harvest Salad

Yield: Serves 4 to 6 | Prep Time: 10 minutes | Cook Time: 20 minutes

Whether you have an at-home garden that's bursting with fall produce or you have fall fever long into the new year, this seasonal salad is a colorful addition to your Thanksgiving spread, providing a new twist of excitement among the traditional dishes. The dressing highlights the natural sweetness of the apples and acorn squash.

INGREDIENTS

Pumpkin Goddess Dressing

1 cup plain Greek yogurt

½ cup sour cream

⅓ cup canned pumpkin

2 tablespoons champagne vinegar

2 tablespoons olive oil

1 tablespoon maple syrup

1 teaspoon minced garlic

½ teaspoon salt

¼ teaspoon ground cinnamon

Salad

1 acorn squash

2 tablespoons olive oil

1 tablespoon salt

1 (5–6-ounce) package baby kale without stems

10 to 12 Brussels sprouts, halved and blanched (see note)

1 Granny Smith apple, cored and cut into matchsticks

½ cup pecans

¼ cup dried cranberries

DIRECTIONS

1. *For the pumpkin goddess dressing:* Process all the ingredients in a blender until well combined. Refrigerate until ready to use.

2. *For the salad:* Preheat the oven to 400°F. Coat a baking sheet with cooking spray and set aside.

3. Slice the squash lengthwise, remove the seeds, and slice horizontally into ½-inch thick rounds. Place the sliced squash on the baking sheet. Drizzle with oil, sprinkle with salt, and toss the squash to coat. Then arrange in a single layer.

4. Bake the squash for about 20 minutes (or until tender and caramelized), flipping halfway through baking.

5. Once the squash has cooled, cut it into bite-size pieces and transfer to a large salad bowl. Add the kale, Brussels sprouts, apple, pecans, and cranberries. Drizzle the dressing over the top and toss gently to mix. Serve immediately.

NOTES

To blanch the Brussels sprouts: Bring a small pot of water to a boil. Add the halved Brussels sprouts and cook for 5 minutes. Remove the sprouts and transfer to a bowl of ice water. Heat 2 tablespoons olive oil in a medium skillet over medium-high heat. Drain the Brussels sprouts, add them to the skillet, and stir to coat with the oil. Cook for 3 minutes and season with salt and pepper.

Creamed Kale

Yield: Serves 6 to 8 | Prep Time: 10 minutes | Cook Time: 15 minutes

Kale is one of the healthiest foods around, full of iron, vitamins A and C, and calcium. While you're stuffing yourself full of turkey, potatoes, pie, and more, it's nice to have this fun, nutrient-rich twist on the more traditional creamed spinach to balance the scales.

INGREDIENTS

1 tablespoon unsalted butter

1 tablespoon extra-virgin olive oil

2 small shallots, sliced

4 garlic cloves, minced

1 (8-ounce) package cream cheese

2 large bunches kale, stemmed, chopped, and lightly steamed

⅓ cup Parmesan cheese

⅓ to ½ cup whole milk

Kosher salt and freshly ground black pepper

DIRECTIONS

1. In a large skillet, heat the butter and oil over medium heat. Once the butter has melted, add the shallots and garlic. Sauté until soft and fragrant, 5 to 7 minutes. Add the cream cheese, break up with a spatula, and let it melt into the pan. Once the cream cheese is mostly melted, add the steamed kale and stir for 3 to 5 minutes. The kale will wilt quickly. Stir in the Parmesan cheese.

2. Add ⅓ cup milk, stir, and add more milk if needed for creaminess and moisture. Season with salt and pepper to taste, and serve.

NOTES

To steam the kale, bring a pot of water to a boil. Add the kale, cover, and steam for 7 to 10 minutes.

Grandma's Southern Corn Pudding

Yield: Serves 8 | Prep Time: 5 minutes | Cook Time: 1 hour

Corn pudding is a favorite in the South and the Midwest, and it's especially welcome during Thanksgiving. The sour cream adds a velvety texture to the pudding that makes it melt-in-your-mouth good. I prefer to use Jiffy cornbread mix in this recipe.

INGREDIENTS

8 tablespoons (1 stick) unsalted butter

1 (8.25-ounce) can creamed corn

1 (8.25-ounce) can whole corn kernels, drained

1 cup finely chopped scallions, including some of the tender green tops

1 cup sour cream

1 large egg

1 (8-ounce) package cornbread mix

DIRECTIONS

1. Preheat the oven to 350°F. Coat a deep-dish pie plate or 8 × 8-inch baking dish with cooking spray.

2. Put the butter in a large microwave-safe bowl and microwave until melted, about 1 minute.

3. Stir in the creamed corn, whole corn kernels, scallions, and sour cream. Add the egg and mix well. Add the cornbread mix and stir just until no dry mix remains—do not overmix.

4. Pour the batter into the baking dish and cook for about 1 hour, until beginning to brown around the edges and a toothpick inserted in the center comes out clean. Cut into triangles or squares and serve.

Baked Mac and Cheese Casserole

Yield: Serves 10 to 12 | Prep Time: 20 minutes | Cook Time: 45 to 55 minutes

One of my cousins was such a picky eater as a kid that during the holidays, he would refuse to eat anything other than mashed potatoes and mac and cheese. He still loves this recipe today because the roux makes the cheese sauce thicker than the kind you'd get out of the box, and the hint of cayenne pepper gives the dish a slightly smoky taste.

INGREDIENTS

1 pound elbow macaroni

1 teaspoon salt, plus extra for the macaroni

4 tablespoons unsalted butter

¼ cup all-purpose flour

½ teaspoon cayenne pepper

3 cups whole milk (or 2 cups whole milk and 1 cup half-and-half)

1 (8-ounce) package cream cheese, room temperature, cut into 1-inch cubes

1 pound processed cheese (such as Velveeta), cut into 1-inch cubes

2 cups shredded cheddar cheese

Fresh sage leaves

DIRECTIONS

1. Preheat the oven to 350°F. Coat a 9 × 13-inch baking dish with cooking spray.

2. Bring a large pot of water to a boil. Add the elbow macaroni and salt and cook until al dente. Drain and reserve.

3. In the same pot, melt the butter over medium-high heat and stir in the flour, 1 teaspoon salt, and cayenne pepper until it is absorbed and light yellow bubbles form, stirring constantly with a wire whisk. Slowly add the milk, whisking constantly until the mixture thickens and bubbles form, about 4 minutes.

4. Add the cream cheese cubes and whisk until no lumps remain. Then add the processed cheese and whisk until completely melted. Remove from the heat and stir in the cooled pasta and 1 cup of the cheddar cheese. Spoon into the baking dish and top with the remaining cheddar cheese. Bake for 30 to 40 minutes. Garnish with sage. Serve.

Broccoli-Rice Casserole

Yield: Serves 8 to 10 | Prep Time: 10 minutes | Cook Time: 30 minutes

While I love to cook holiday meals from scratch, when I'm juggling various sides and desserts with the main course, I need to have a few shortcut recipes, like this one, up my sleeve. By using canned soup and frozen broccoli, I save myself a lot of prep time, so I can tend to everything else.

INGREDIENTS

2 tablespoons unsalted butter

1 cup finely diced onion

1 cup finely diced celery

1 teaspoon salt

½ teaspoon freshly ground black pepper

½ teaspoon paprika

1 pound processed cheese (such as Velveeta), cut into 1-inch cubes

2 (10.75-ounce) cans cream of celery soup or cheddar cheese soup

2½ cups instant rice (such as Minute Rice)

1 cup half-and-half

12 ounces frozen broccoli florets, thawed

½ cup shredded cheddar cheese

DIRECTIONS

1. Preheat the oven to 350° F. Coat a 9 × 13-inch baking dish with cooking spray.

2. In a large saucepan, melt the butter over medium heat. Add the onion and celery, stirring until the vegetables are translucent, about 2 minutes. Add the salt, pepper, and paprika and stir for another minute. Add the processed cheese and cream of celery soup, lower the heat to medium-low, and stir until the cheese melts.

3. Add the instant rice, half-and-half, and all but 1 cup of the broccoli and stir until well mixed.

4. Spoon the mixture into the baking dish and arrange the remaining broccoli on top in decorative rows, then sprinkle cheddar cheese between the rows.

5. Bake for 30 minutes, until the cheese is melted and the casserole is heated through. Serve.

Green Bean Casserole

Yield: Serves 6 to 8 | Prep Time: 10 minutes | Cook Time: 40 minutes

The green bean casserole is the ultimate company-ready side dish. This version is particularly appealing because of the sautéed mushrooms and crunchy French fried onion topping.

INGREDIENTS

1 pound green beans, ends trimmed

1 teaspoon salt, plus extra for boiling the green beans

2 tablespoons unsalted butter

1 garlic clove, minced

1 shallot, sliced

6 ounces cremini mushrooms, trimmed and chopped

1 teaspoon freshly ground black pepper

2 tablespoons all-purpose flour

1 cup chicken broth

1 cup half-and-half

1 tablespoon Worcestershire sauce

1 (6-ounce) can crispy fried onions

DIRECTIONS

1. Preheat the oven to 375°F. Coat a 9 × 13-inch baking dish with cooking spray and set aside. Prepare a large bowl of ice water.

2. Bring a large pot of water to a boil. Add the green beans and a generous amount of salt and boil for 5 minutes. Drain the beans and immediately immerse in the ice water to stop the cooking process. Drain again and set aside.

3. In a large, deep skillet, heat the butter over medium-high heat. Add the garlic and shallots, stirring occasionally, until the shallots begin to soften, about 5 minutes. Add the mushrooms, 1 teaspoon salt, and pepper and cook for 1 to 2 minutes. Sprinkle in the flour and stir to combine. Cook for 2 minutes. Add the chicken broth and stir to combine. Then add the half-and-half and simmer until the mixture thickens, stirring occasionally, for 6 to 8 minutes. Stir in the Worcestershire sauce.

4. Remove from the heat and stir in all of the green beans. Transfer the green bean mixture to the baking dish. Top with the fried onions.

5. Bake for about 20 minutes, until bubbling. Serve immediately.

Candied Yams

Yield: Serves 8 | Prep Time: 10 minutes | Cook Time: 60 to 65 minutes

The combination of cinnamon, nutmeg, and honey in the sauce is especially enticing and complements the dish to perfection. I've even reused this sauce for other dishes, like ice cream or pumpkin pie.

INGREDIENTS

1½ pounds yams, sliced ⅛-inch thick (or sweet potatoes)

8 tablespoons unsalted butter

1 cup sugar

¼ cup heavy cream

2½ to 3 teaspoons ground cinnamon

½ teaspoon grated nutmeg

2 tablespoons honey

DIRECTIONS

1. Preheat the oven to 350°F. Coat a 9 × 13-inch baking dish with cooking spray.

2. Place the yams into the baking dish and set aside.

3. In a medium pot, melt the butter over medium heat. Add the sugar and stir until well blended. Add the cream and stir until creamy. Stir in the cinnamon, nutmeg, and honey. Pour the mixture over the yams. Cover with aluminum foil and bake for 40 minutes.

4. Remove the foil and bake for an additional 20 to 25 minutes. Serve immediately, spooning the syrupy sauce over the yams.

Slow Cooker Rosemary Dinner Rolls

Yield: Makes 12 rolls | Prep Time: 20 to 30 minutes | Cook Time: 1 hour on low, plus 1 hour on high

When the holidays come around, I try to search for recipes that'll use every inch of the kitchen, which is why I love that these rolls are made in the slow cooker. When you've already got a turkey in the oven and a couple of casseroles to reheat, here's how you can enjoy fresh-baked bread without using the oven.

INGREDIENTS

2¼ teaspoons active dry yeast

½ cup warm water (110°F)

½ cup whole milk, room temperature

1 large egg, room temperature

2 tablespoons olive oil

2 teaspoons sugar

1½ teaspoons kosher salt

3 cups all-purpose flour, plus extra as needed

¼ cup grated Parmesan cheese

1½ tablespoons chopped fresh rosemary

1 teaspoon garlic powder

2 tablespoons unsalted butter, melted

DIRECTIONS

1. In a small bowl, stir the yeast into the warm water until dissolved. Let stand until the mixture is foamy, 5 to 10 minutes.

2. Using a stand mixer fitted with the paddle attachment, beat the milk, egg, oil, sugar, and salt on medium speed until combined, about 3 minutes. With the mixer running, slowly add the yeast mixture, then add the flour, 2 tablespoons cheese, the rosemary, and garlic powder and beat until combined.

3. Switch to the dough hook and knead for 5 to 9 minutes on low speed, until the dough is slightly tacky, but smooth. Add a bit more flour if the dough is too sticky. Turn the dough out onto a lightly floured work surface. Using a sharp knife, slice the dough into 12 even pieces. Roll each piece into a ball.

4. Line a 6-quart slow cooker insert with 2 pieces of parchment paper and lightly coat the parchment paper with cooking spray. Place the balls of dough in the slow cooker on top of the parchment paper. (A 6-quart slow cooker can fit 12 rolls side by side.)

5. Cover and cook for 1 hour on low. Switch to high and cook for 1 more hour. Preheat the broiler.

6. Lift the rolls from the slow cooker using the parchment paper. Remove rolls from the parchment paper and place them on a baking sheet. Brush with melted butter and 2 tablespoons cheese and broil for 3 to 5 minutes until golden on top. Serve.

Cranberry Sauce

Yield: Serves 6 to 8 | Prep Time: 5 minutes | Cook Time: 15 minutes

Cranberry sauce is essential to the perfect Thanksgiving dinner, and this three-ingredient recipe is so simple that I can whip it up while the turkey is resting. Add the larger amount of sugar if you prefer a sweeter sauce.

INGREDIENTS

1 (12-ounce) package fresh cranberries, rinsed and drained

1 orange, peeled, segmented and each segment cut in half

¾ to 1 cup sugar

Candied lemon

DIRECTIONS

1. Place half of the cranberries and half of the orange pieces in a food processor. Pulse until the mixture is evenly chopped. Transfer to a medium saucepan. Repeat with the remaining cranberries (reserving a few for garnish) and orange pieces. Stir in the sugar.

2. Bring the mixture to a boil over medium-high heat. Reduce the heat to medium-low and simmer until the mixture becomes a vibrant red and the sugar is dissolved, about 15 minutes.

3. Transfer to a dish and let cool. Garnish with candied lemon and reserved cranberries, if desired. Refrigerate until ready to serve. (The sauce will thicken as it cools.)

Scalloped Potatoes

Yield: Serves 6 to 8 | Prep Time: 20 minutes | Cook Time: 40 minutes

They're creamy. They're cheesy. And they're a staple of the holiday season. Christmas dinner just isn't complete without a heaping mound of scalloped potatoes on your plate. The Gruyère cheese adds a slightly nutty taste to the potatoes.

INGREDIENTS

2 pounds Yukon Gold potatoes, peeled and sliced ⅛ inch thick

Salt and freshly ground black pepper

2½ cups shredded Gruyère cheese

½ cup grated Parmesan cheese

3 tablespoons unsalted butter, cut into small pieces

2½ cups half-and-half

Fresh thyme, chopped

DIRECTIONS

1. Preheat the oven to 350°F. Coat a 9 × 13-inch baking dish with cooking spray.

2. Spread an even layer of potatoes on the bottom of the baking dish. Season with salt and pepper. Spread half of the Gruyère cheese and half of the Parmesan cheese evenly over the potatoes and dot with half of the butter.

3. Top with any remaining potatoes. Pour the half-and-half evenly over the cheese. Top with the remaining Gruyère, Parmesan, and butter.

4. Cover the dish with aluminum foil and bake for 30 minutes. Remove the foil and bake for an additional 10 minutes until the top is bubbling and golden brown. Let cool for 10 to 15 minutes. The sauce will thicken as it cools. Sprinkle with thyme and serve.

Herb-Roasted Potatoes

Yield: Serves 6 to 8 | Prep Time: 15 minutes | Cook Time: 30 minutes

These potatoes are like that staple piece of your wardrobe that you can dress up to wear to an art gallery opening or dress down for a chill night with friends. They pair well with everything from The Best Roast Turkey (page 79) on Thanksgiving to Company-Ready Brisket (page 91) for Hanukkah or Christmas.

INGREDIENTS

3½ to 4 pounds Yukon Gold potatoes, unpeeled, scrubbed

¼ cup olive oil

1 teaspoon kosher salt

1 teaspoon herbes de Provence

DIRECTIONS

1. Preheat the oven to 425°F. Generously coat a baking sheet with cooking spray.

2. Cut the potatoes evenly into 1- to 2-inch pieces. Place them on the prepared baking sheet, drizzle with the oil, and sprinkle with the salt and herbes de Provence. Toss gently to evenly distribute the ingredients and then arrange the pieces skin-side down.

3. Place the baking sheet in the middle of the oven and bake for 30 minutes, or until brown and slightly puffed. Transfer to a platter and serve.

Hanukkah Potato Latkes

Yield: Makes 12 to 15 latkes | Prep Time: 30 to 40 minutes | Cook Time: 10 to 15 minutes

Potato latkes are another traditional treat to celebrate the miracle of oil on your Hanukkah menu. You can serve these up as a side dish during dinner, or you can serve them in the morning for a potato-based breakfast.

INGREDIENTS

1 pound Yukon Gold potatoes, peeled

½ cup finely grated onion

1 large egg, lightly beaten

3 tablespoons finely chopped fresh flat-leaf parsley

½ teaspoon salt, plus extra for seasoning

½ teaspoon freshly ground black pepper

½ to ¾ cup vegetable oil

DIRECTIONS

1. Coarsely grate the potatoes with a box grater. Soak the potatoes and onion in cold water for 5 minutes, then drain well in a colander.

2. Spread the grated potatoes and onion on a clean tea towel. Twist the towel tightly to wring out as much liquid as possible. Transfer the potato mixture to a large bowl and stir in the egg, parsley, salt, and pepper.

3. In a large nonstick skillet, heat ¼ cup of the oil over medium-high heat. Spoon the potato mixture into the skillet in 4 places, using about 2 tablespoons mixture per latke, and spread them into 3-inch rounds with a fork. Cook for 2 to 3 minutes, until brown. Turn the latkes over and cook for an additional 2 to 3 minutes, until the second side is brown. Transfer to paper towels to drain and season with salt. Repeat with the remaining potato mixture, using additional oil as necessary. Serve.

Slow Cooker Chunky Applesauce

Yield: Serves 12 | Prep Time: 20 minutes | Cook Time: 6 to 8 hours on low

Applesauce is one of those versatile holiday dishes that always seems to come in handy. You can make some to serve on the side of the Hanukkah Potato Latkes (page 124) or serve it alongside your Thanksgiving or Christmas dinner spread for the kids to enjoy.

INGREDIENTS

10 Granny Smith apples, peeled, cored, and cut into chunks

1 cup sugar

½ cup apple juice

2 teaspoons ground cinnamon

DIRECTIONS

1. Put the apples, sugar, apple juice, and cinnamon in a 6-quart slow cooker. Stir to mix well. Cover and cook on low for 6 to 8 hours, until tender, stirring occasionally.

2. Remove from the slow cooker, stir to your desired consistency, and let come to room temperature. (The mixture will thicken as it cools.) Serve at room temperature or refrigerate and serve cold.

Noodle Kugel

Yield: Serves 8 to 12 | Prep Time: 20 minutes | Cook Time: 1 hour 10 minutes

The smattering of golden raisins throughout this kugel dish has to be the most memorable part. It adds an interesting dynamic in both texture and taste, with small bursts of sweetness shining through the rich pudding.

INGREDIENTS

1 cup golden raisins

12 ounces broad egg noodles

6 large eggs

2 cups sour cream

1 cup cottage cheese

1 (8-ounce) package cream cheese, softened

1 cup sugar, plus extra for the topping

4 tablespoons unsalted butter, melted

½ teaspoon vanilla extract

½ teaspoon ground cinnamon, plus extra for the topping

¼ teaspoon salt

DIRECTIONS

1. Preheat the oven to 350°F. Coat a 9 × 13-inch baking dish with cooking spray.

2. In a small bowl, cover the raisins with hot tap water and let soak while preparing the remaining ingredients.

3. Bring a large pot of water to a boil. Add the egg noodles and cook until al dente. Drain and return to the pot.

4. Meanwhile, combine the eggs, sour cream, cottage cheese, cream cheese, sugar, melted butter, vanilla, cinnamon, and salt in a blender and blend until smooth and creamy. Pour the egg mixture over the noodles and stir to combine.

5. Drain the raisins and stir into the noodle mixture. Pour the mixture into the baking dish. Sprinkle lightly with extra cinnamon and generously with extra sugar.

6. Bake for 1 hour, until the center of the kugel is set, and the noodles begin to turn golden brown.

7. Let rest for 20 minutes before cutting. Serve warm or refrigerate and serve cold.

Hanukkah Challah Bread

Yield: Makes 1 very large loaf | Prep Time: 20 minutes, plus 2½ hours rising time | Cook Time: 30 minutes

Challah bread is a mainstay during Jewish holidays and the Sabbath, and this traditional recipe is a fun alternative to buying a loaf from the bakery. If you wish, feel free to add raisins or sprinkle poppy seeds on top to customize the loaf to your taste!

INGREDIENTS

2 tablespoons warm water (110°F), plus 1 tablespoon cold water

¼ cup sugar

2 teaspoons active dry yeast

3 large eggs

¼ cup vegetable oil, plus extra for the bowl

4 cups all-purpose flour, plus extra as needed

2 teaspoons salt

DIRECTIONS

1. In a small bowl, combine 2 tablespoons warm water, 1 teaspoon sugar, and the yeast. Let stand until the mixture is foamy, about 5 minutes. Separate 1 egg and reserve the white. Whisk the yolk with the 2 remaining eggs in a separate bowl, then whisk in the oil.

2. Using a stand mixer fitted with the paddle attachment, mix the flour, salt, and remaining sugar on low speed for 20 seconds until combined. Increase the speed to medium, add the egg mixture, and beat for 2 minutes. Turn off the mixer and scrape down the bowl. Add the yeast mixture and beat until incorporated. Change to the dough hook, reduce the speed to low, and knead for 6 to 8 minutes, until the dough is smooth. Oil a large bowl and place the ball of dough into it. Cover tightly with plastic wrap and let rise in a warm place until doubled in size, about 1½ hours.

3. Transfer the dough to a lightly floured work surface and divide into 3 equal portions. Roll and pull each portion into a 14-inch rope. Lay the 3 ropes side by side on a large sheet of parchment paper with the ends facing you. Pinch the tops together and then gently braid the 3 ropes, pinching the ends together and tucking them under to seal. Tuck the sides in a bit to make a plump, tightly braided loaf. Use the parchment paper to slide the loaf onto a large baking sheet, cover the dough with a tea towel, and let rise for 1 hour.

4. Preheat the oven to 350°F. Use a fork to beat the reserved egg white with the cold water. With a pastry brush, spread the egg white mixture all over the loaf, including into the seams and down the sides. Bake for 30 minutes, or until the top is golden brown and the internal temperature is 190°F.

5. Let the loaf cool completely on a wire rack before slicing and serving.

Twice-Baked Sweet Potatoes

Yield: Serves 2 | Prep Time: 20 minutes | Cook Time: 35 to 45 minutes

Sweet potatoes are a mainstay during the holidays. The cream cheese adds a creamier, sweeter punch to an already sweet veggie. Baking them twice gives them a slightly crispy edge that makes for a fun alternative to the traditional mashed version.

INGREDIENTS

2 large sweet potatoes, unpeeled

2 ounces cream cheese

2 tablespoons heavy cream

1 tablespoon light brown sugar

¼ teaspoon ground cinnamon

¼ cup chopped pecans

Salt and freshly ground black pepper

Fresh parsley leaves

DIRECTIONS

1. Preheat the oven to 425° F. Line a baking sheet with aluminum foil.

2. Cut the potatoes lengthwise in half and place cut-side down on the baking sheet. Bake until tender, 30 to 35 minutes.

3. Scoop out the centers of the potatoes into a medium bowl, leaving ¼-inch-thick shells. Add the cream cheese, cream, brown sugar, and cinnamon to the potato centers and mash until combined.

4. Fill the sweet potato shells with the potato mixture; sprinkle with the pecans and season with salt and pepper. Return to the oven and bake until the potatoes are heated through and the pecans are toasted, 5 to 8 minutes. Sprinkle with parsley and serve.

Southern Cornbread Dressing

Yield: Serves 12 | Prep Time: 30 minutes | Cook Time: 40 to 60 minutes

I love using this particular recipe because the buttermilk makes the cornbread extra creamy. I recommend making the cornbread from scratch, but if you're in a rush, you can use ready-made cornbread from the grocery store bakery.

INGREDIENTS

Buttermilk Cornbread

2 cups buttermilk

2 cups cornmeal

1 cup self-rising flour

2 large eggs

1 tablespoon unsalted butter

Cornbread Dressing

3 slices white bread or 3 store-bought buttermilk biscuits

1 onion, diced

1 cup diced celery

1 cup canned cream of chicken soup

3 large eggs

6 tablespoons unsalted butter, sliced

1 teaspoon kosher salt

1 teaspoon freshly ground black pepper

1 teaspoon rubbed sage

4 to 5 cups chicken broth

DIRECTIONS

1. *For the buttermilk cornbread:* Place a 10½-inch cast-iron skillet in the oven and preheat the oven to 425°F.

2. In a medium bowl, combine the buttermilk, cornmeal, flour, eggs, and ½ cup water.

3. When the oven has reached 425°F, remove the skillet and add the butter; let melt. Pour the cornbread batter into the skillet and bake for 10 to 15 minutes, until set. Let cool.

4. *For the cornbread dressing:* Lower the oven temperature to 350°F. Coat two 9 × 13-inch baking dishes with cooking spray.

5. In a large bowl, crumble the cooled cornbread and white bread. Add the onion, celery, soup, eggs, butter, salt, pepper, and sage, then pour 4 cups of the broth over the mixture and stir to combine. Add the remaining broth as needed if the dressing looks too dry.

6. Divide the dressing into the 2 baking dishes. Bake for 30 to 45 minutes, until light brown and set. Serve.

The Best Broccoli Salad

Yield: Serves 6 to 8 | Prep Time: 15 minutes | Chill Time: 2 hours

This broccoli salad tends to get gobbled up as soon as it's been set on the table. It plays with so many different textures, from the chewy raisins to the crunchy cashews and soft cubes of cheese, which is what makes it so popular.

INGREDIENTS

Dressing

¾ cup mayonnaise

¼ cup sugar

1 tablespoon balsamic vinegar

Salad

1½ pounds broccoli, chopped into bite-size pieces

1 cup raisins

¾ cup cashew pieces

1 small shallot, finely chopped (about ¼ cup)

4 ounces cheddar cheese, cut into bite-size cubes (1 cup)

6 slices bacon, cooked and crumbled

DIRECTIONS

1. *For the dressing:* In a small bowl, whisk together the mayonnaise, sugar, and vinegar. Set aside.

2. *For the salad:* In a large bowl, toss the broccoli, raisins, cashews, shallot, cheese cubes, and bacon together. Pour the dressing over the broccoli mixture and toss to coat all of the ingredients with the sauce.

3. Cover with plastic wrap and refrigerate for 2 hours. Serve.

Brown Sugar–Bourbon Glazed Carrots

Yield: Serves 6 | Prep Time: 5 minutes | Cook Time: 20 to 25 minutes

The light bourbon glaze adds a sweetness to the carrots that will have everyone clamoring to load up on more vegetables.

INGREDIENTS

8 tablespoons unsalted butter

1 pound baby carrots

Grated zest and juice of 1 orange

½ teaspoon salt

¼ cup bourbon

¼ cup packed light brown sugar

Fresh parsley, for garnish

DIRECTIONS

1. In a large heavy-bottomed skillet, melt the butter over medium heat. Add the carrots, orange juice, and salt. Cover and simmer gently for 10 minutes, or until the baby carrots are just fork-tender.

2. Remove the pan from the heat and carefully add the bourbon and brown sugar. Return the pan to the heat and continue simmering, uncovered, until the sauce has reduced by half and created a syrupy glaze. Toss with the orange zest and transfer to a serving dish. Garnish with parsley and serve immediately.

Holiday Peas

Yield: Serves 6 to 8　│　Prep Time: 5 minutes　│　Cook Time: 15 minutes

These peas work especially well alongside the Olive Oil Roast with Red Wine Jus (page 88) in your Christmas spread because the mint flavor is in keeping with the tastes of the season.

INGREDIENTS

2 (10-ounce) packages frozen peas

2 tablespoons unsalted butter

2 tablespoons all-purpose flour

Salt and freshly ground black pepper

¾ cup whole milk

¼ cup coarsely chopped fresh mint

Fresh parsley, for garnish

DIRECTIONS

1. Cook the peas according to the package directions.

2. In a medium saucepan, melt the butter. Whisk in the flour, ½ teaspoon salt, and ¼ teaspoon pepper until blended and beginning to bubble. Slowly whisk the milk into the mixture and bring to a boil. Cook and stir for 1 to 2 minutes, or until thickened. Taste and adjust the seasonings as needed.

3. Drain the peas and mix into the sauce. Add the mint and stir. Transfer to a serving dish, garnish with parsley, and serve.

Cinnamon-Roasted Butternut Squash

Yield: Serves 4 to 6 | Prep Time: 10 minutes | Cook Time: 20 minutes

I love putting seasonal produce to work during the holidays, and this winter squash recipe allows me to do exactly that. Plus, you can save the seeds to roast later as a snack.

INGREDIENTS

1 (1½–2 pound) butternut squash, peeled, seeded, and cubed

¼ cup light brown sugar (not packed)

2 tablespoons ground cinnamon

2 tablespoons olive oil

Salt

Fresh thyme, for garnish

DIRECTIONS

1. Preheat the oven to 375°F. Coat a baking sheet with cooking spray.

2. Scatter the squash cubes on the sheet. Sprinkle with the brown sugar and cinnamon, drizzle with the oil, and season with salt. Bake for 20 minutes, or until the squash is golden brown and tender.

3. Let cool for 5 minutes. Adjust the seasoning, if needed. Spoon into a serving bowl, garnish with thyme, and serve.

Cranberry-Pecan Brussels Sprouts

Yield: Serves 4 to 6 | Prep Time: 10 minutes | Cook Time: 30 minutes

I'm so glad to see that in recent years, tasty Brussels sprouts are finally getting their due. Dried cranberries, pecans, and a dash of nutmeg turn this year-round favorite vegetable into a Christmas classic. The red, dried cranberries paired against the green Brussels sprouts especially befit the holiday season.

INGREDIENTS

1 pound Brussels sprouts, trimmed and halved

½ cup dried cranberries

½ cup pecans (whole or chopped)

½ small red onion, thinly sliced

2 tablespoons olive oil

Salt and freshly ground black pepper

Freshly grated nutmeg

DIRECTIONS

1. Preheat the oven to 375°F. Coat a baking sheet with cooking spray.

2. Scatter the Brussels sprouts, dried cranberries, pecans, and red onion evenly across the baking sheet. Drizzle with the oil, and season with salt and pepper. Bake for 30 minutes, or until the Brussels sprouts are golden and slightly tender.

3. Sprinkle the nutmeg lightly over the Brussels sprouts, transfer to a serving bowl, and serve immediately.

5

Desserts

With a homemade pie or cake and a freshly brewed drink
in hand, your holiday evening winds down to a comforting,
satisfying end. Lazy games of Scrabble are played over slices of
pumpkin pie (page 150), the quiet murmur of football playing in
the background, around Thanksgiving. And during Christmas,
everyone gets back in their pajamas as they enjoy homemade
fudge (page 185) or cheesecake brownies (page 182).

Upside-Down Apple Pie

Yield: Serves 6 to 8 | Prep Time: 20 minutes | Cook Time: 1 hour to 1 hour, 15 minutes

Apples are royalty in the world of fall fruits. And even though they're everywhere, it's impossible to get tired of them. This Upside-Down Apple Pie puts a fun twist on an all-American fall favorite, so you can celebrate the flavors of the season in style. It's a great recipe to make with kids!

INGREDIENTS

¾ cup packed light brown sugar

½ cup pecan halves

6 tablespoons unsalted butter, melted

Pie dough for 1 double-crust 9-inch pie (store-bought or homemade)

1 cup granulated sugar

⅓ cup all-purpose flour

¾ teaspoon ground cinnamon

5 large Granny Smith or other firm apples, peeled, cored, and cut into ½-inch wedges

DIRECTIONS

1. Preheat the oven to 375°F. Coat a 9-inch deep-dish pie plate with cooking spray and line it with wax paper. Coat the wax paper with cooking spray.

2. In a small bowl, combine the brown sugar, pecans, and 4 tablespoons of the melted butter; mix well and spread evenly over the bottom of the pie plate. Roll out the bottom crust and place it in the pie plate, pressing the crust firmly against the nut mixture and the sides of the pie plate; set aside.

3. In a large bowl, combine the granulated sugar, flour, cinnamon, and remaining 2 tablespoons melted butter; mix well. Add the apples and toss gently to coat. Spoon into the pie crust.

4. Roll out the top crust and place it over the apple mixture. Trim and fold the edges together to seal. Using a knife, cut four 1-inch slits in the top crust. Bake for 1 to 1¼ hours, until the crust is golden.

5. Carefully loosen the wax paper around the rim and invert the pie onto a serving plate while still hot. Remove the wax paper and let cool slightly. Slice and serve warm, or let cool completely before serving.

Foolproof Pumpkin Pie

Yield: Serves 6 to 8 | Prep Time: 30 minutes | Cook Time: 50 to 55 minutes

What's Thanksgiving without pumpkin pie? This traditional, made-from-scratch recipe is just like the pies you remember from your childhood; however, the bourbon whipped cream gives it an exciting new twist. You can make extra to serve with the Upside-Down Apple Pie (page 149) or Triple Berry Pie (page 153)!

INGREDIENTS

Pumpkin Pie

1 (9-inch) pie crust (store-bought or homemade), plus extra pie dough for decoration, if desired

2 cups canned pumpkin puree

1¼ cups evaporated milk

3 large eggs, beaten

½ cup granulated sugar

½ cup light brown sugar

1 teaspoon ground cinnamon

½ teaspoon kosher salt

½ teaspoon ground ginger

½ teaspoon grated nutmeg

¼ teaspoon ground cloves

¼ teaspoon ground cardamom

Bourbon Whipped Cream

1 cup heavy cream

2 tablespoons powdered sugar

1½ tablespoons bourbon

DIRECTIONS

1. *For the pumpkin pie:* Place the pie crust in the refrigerator while preparing the filling. Preheat the oven to 425°F.

2. In a medium bowl, whisk the pumpkin puree, evaporated milk, eggs, granulated sugar, brown sugar, cinnamon, salt, ginger, nutmeg, cloves, and cardamom until combined.

3. Pour the filling into the pie crust. Cut out fun shapes with the extra pie dough, if desired, and lay decoratively on top of the pie. Bake for 15 minutes. Lower the oven temperature to 350°F and bake for an additional 35 to 40 minutes, or until the center of the pie jiggles slightly and the filling is set. Let cool completely on a wire rack.

4. *For the bourbon whipped cream:* While the pie is cooling, whip the cream to medium stiff peaks. Slowly add the powdered sugar. Fold in the bourbon. Refrigerate until the pie is cool, then slice the pie and serve with the whipped cream.

Triple Berry Pie

Yield: Serves 6 to 8 | Prep Time: 30 minutes | Cook Time: 50 to 55 minutes

I love this pie because it just looks so darn pretty! The soft red raspberries contrast nicely with the darker blueberries and blackberries. You can do all sorts of fun things with the crust—try a lattice top or even make fun seasonal punch-outs with cookie cutters.

INGREDIENTS

Pie dough for 1 double-crust 9-inch pie (store-bought or homemade)

7 cups fresh or thawed frozen raspberries, blueberries, and blackberries

1 cup granulated sugar, plus extra as needed

1 teaspoon grated lemon zest plus 1 tablespoon lemon juice

¼ teaspoon kosher salt

½ teaspoon ground cinnamon

¼ cup cornstarch

2 tablespoons unsalted butter

1 large egg, beaten with a little water

1 tablespoon sanding sugar

DIRECTIONS

1. Preheat the oven to 400°F.

2. Roll out the bottom crust and place it in a 9-inch pie plate; refrigerate while preparing the filling.

3. In a large saucepan, combine the berries, granulated sugar, lemon zest and juice, salt, and cinnamon and cook over medium heat. Simmer until the berries are warm and juicy, about 8 minutes. Taste and add more sugar if needed.

4. Transfer ½ cup of the juice to a small bowl. Stir in the cornstarch until smooth. Pour the cornstarch mixture back into the pot with the berries and gently stir and cook for 2 to 5 minutes, until the mixture thickens. Remove from the heat and add the butter.

5. Pour the berry filling into the pie shell. Roll out the top crust and either cut into strips to form a lattice crust or cut slits or holes for steam to escape. Place the top crust over the filling, pinch the edges of the top and bottom crusts, and then crimp the edges together. Brush the top with the egg wash and sprinkle with sanding sugar.

6. Bake for 40 to 45 minutes, until the filling is bubbling and the crust is golden brown. After 30 minutes, check the pie, and if the crust is browning too fast, cover loosely with a piece of aluminum foil. Let cool completely on a wire rack. Slice and serve.

Cran-Apple and Pecan Lattice Pie

Yield: Serves 6 to 8 | Prep Time: 20 minutes | Cook Time: 45 to 60 minutes

This is the ultimate end-of-the-year pie, packed with all of the flavors of the season from cranberries to apples to pecans. The decorative lattice crust is as fun to make as it is pretty to look at.

INGREDIENTS

Pie dough for 1 double-crust 9-inch pie (store-bought or homemade)

1⅓ pounds apples, peeled, cored, and sliced (4 cups)

2 cups cranberries

1 cup pecans

¾ cup granulated sugar

1 tablespoon cornstarch

1 teaspoon ground cinnamon

2 tablespoons unsalted butter, cut into small pieces

DIRECTIONS

1. Preheat the oven to 400°F.

2. Roll out the bottom crust and place it in a 9-inch pie plate; add the apples. Spread the cranberries over the apples and top with the pecans. In a small bowl, whisk together the sugar, cornstarch, and cinnamon and sprinkle the mixture over the fruit and nuts. Distribute the butter pieces over the pie filling.

3. Roll out the top crust to a 10 × 12-inch rectangle and cut lengthwise into 18 long, narrow strips. Arrange the strips over the filling, seven horizontally and seven vertically in a lattice pattern. Arrange the four remaining strips around the edge of the pie plate. Tuck the ends under the edge of the bottom crust and then crimp the crusts together.

4. Bake until the pie is browned and the fruit filling is bubbling, 45 minutes to 1 hour. Let cool for 5 minutes on a wire rack before slicing and serving.

Sweet Potato Pie

Yield: Serves 6 to 8 | Prep Time: 15 minutes | Cook Time: 45 minutes

You can't host a traditional holiday dinner without some sweet potatoes on the side or for dessert. The hint of nutmeg adds a sweet seasonal kick.

INGREDIENTS

1½ pounds sweet potatoes

8 tablespoons butter, softened

½ cup packed light brown sugar

¼ cup dark corn syrup

½ teaspoon grated nutmeg

¼ teaspoon salt

1 (12-ounce) can evaporated milk

2 large eggs

2 teaspoons vanilla extract

1 (9-inch) pie crust (store-bought or homemade)

DIRECTIONS

1. Preheat the oven to 375°F.

2. Scrub the sweet potatoes and microwave for about 7 minutes, or until very soft. Peel away the skins and measure the pulp—you should have 3 cups.

3. Process the pulp and the butter in a food processor until completely smooth. Add the brown sugar, corn syrup, nutmeg, and salt and pulse briefly. Combine the evaporated milk, eggs, and vanilla in a measuring cup and, with the processor running, add to the potato puree until combined.

4. Pour into the prepared crust and bake for about 45 minutes, or until the center is set. Let cool completely, then slice and serve.

Autumn Spice Cake

Yield: Serves 8 | Prep Time: 20 minutes | Cook Time: 30 minutes

It's okay to rebel against pie on Thanksgiving. This spice-filled cake ensures no one will miss it!

INGREDIENTS

Spice Cake

2¼ cups all-purpose flour, plus extra for the pans

1 teaspoon baking powder

1 teaspoon baking soda

½ teaspoon salt

2½ teaspoons ground cinnamon

1 teaspoon grated nutmeg

1 teaspoon ground ginger

½ teaspoon allspice

¼ teaspoon ground cloves

1¾ cups packed light brown sugar

¾ cup vegetable oil

¾ cup unsweetened applesauce

4 large eggs

2 teaspoons vanilla extract

1 cup whole milk

1 cup chopped pecans (optional)

Assorted sprinkles (optional)

Cream Cheese Frosting

12 ounces cream cheese, softened but still cool

8 tablespoons unsalted butter, softened but still cool

3½ cups powdered sugar

½ teaspoon vanilla extract

DIRECTIONS

1. *For the spice cake:* Preheat the oven to 350°F. Coat two 9-inch round cake pans well with cooking spray, then lightly dust with flour and shake out the excess.

2. In a medium bowl, whisk the flour, baking powder, baking soda, salt, cinnamon, nutmeg, ginger, allspice, and cloves.

3. Using a stand mixer fitted with the paddle attachment, beat the brown sugar, oil, and applesauce on medium until combined.

4. Add the eggs and vanilla and beat to combine. Add half of the flour mixture and mix on low until combined. Blend in the milk, then add the remaining flour mixture and mix until combined.

5. Divide the batter between the prepared pans. Bake until a toothpick inserted into the center comes out clean, about 30 minutes. Let cool in the pans for several minutes, then run a knife around the edges and invert onto a wire rack to cool completely.

6. *For the cream cheese frosting:* Using a hand mixer or a stand mixer fitted with the paddle attachment, beat the cream cheese and butter until smooth and creamy. Add the powdered sugar and vanilla and beat until well blended.

7. Level the tops of the cakes as needed. Place a cake layer on a cake plate. Spread some cream cheese frosting over the cake in an even layer. Add the second cake layer and frost the top and sides of the cake. Sprinkle the pecans and sprinkles on top, if desired. Slice and serve.

Easy Pecan Pie Bars

Yield: Makes 36 bars | Prep Time: 15 minutes | Cook Time: 40 to 50 minutes

These pecan pie bars let you vary the dessert style while keeping the tried-and-true flavors of the season, and you can package up leftovers for your guests to take home. Since you don't need to use a fork and knife to eat them, they make an excellent potluck dessert.

INGREDIENTS

⅓ cup granulated sugar

⅓ cup powdered sugar

8 tablespoons unsalted butter, softened

2 teaspoons vanilla extract

1½ cups all-purpose flour

3 large eggs

⅔ cup packed light brown sugar

½ cup corn syrup

¼ teaspoon kosher salt

1 cup coarsely chopped pecans

4 ounces bittersweet or dark chocolate, melted, for drizzling (optional)

DIRECTIONS

1. Preheat the oven to 350°F. Lightly coat a 9 × 13-inch baking dish with cooking spray.

2. In a large bowl, combine the granulated sugar, powdered sugar, butter, and 1 teaspoon of the vanilla and mix well. Stir in the flour. Press the dough mixture evenly in the bottom and up the sides of the baking dish. Bake for 15 to 18 minutes, or until the edges are golden.

3. While the crust is baking, beat the eggs, brown sugar, corn syrup, salt, and remaining 1 teaspoon vanilla in a medium bowl. Stir in the pecans. Pour over the crust and bake for 25 to 30 minutes, until set.

4. Run a knife around the edges of the pan. Let cool for about 1 hour. Drizzle the melted chocolate over the bars, if desired, and let dry. Cut into 36 bars and serve.

Pumpkin Spice Roll

Yield: Serves 8 | Prep Time: 30 minutes | Cook Time: 13 to 15 minutes, plus 1 hour 20 minutes chill time

This unique pinwheel dessert pairs particularly well with after-dinner coffee. I like to cut a few slices beforehand and arrange them on a serving platter. They look so appealing that guests simply can't resist.

INGREDIENTS

Cake

1 cup sugar

¾ cup all-purpose flour

½ teaspoon baking powder

½ teaspoon baking soda

1 teaspoon ground cinnamon

½ teaspoon ground ginger

¼ teaspoon ground cloves

¼ teaspoon grated nutmeg

¼ teaspoon kosher salt

1 cup pumpkin puree

3 large eggs

Filling

1 (8-ounce) package cream cheese, room temperature

4 tablespoons unsalted butter, softened

1 teaspoon vanilla extract

1 cup powdered sugar

Topping

2 tablespoons powdered sugar

¼ teaspoon ground cinnamon

DIRECTIONS

1. *For the cake:* Preheat the oven to 375°F. Lightly coat a rimmed 18 × 13-inch baking sheet with cooking spray. Line with parchment paper.

2. In a large bowl, whisk the sugar, flour, baking powder, baking soda, cinnamon, ginger, cloves, nutmeg, and salt. Add the pumpkin puree and eggs and mix well.

3. Pour the mixture onto the baking sheet. Bake for 13 to 15 minutes, until the cake is set and a toothpick inserted in the middle comes out clean.

4. Remove the cake from the oven and while the cake is still hot, carefully lift up with the parchment from the baking sheet and place on a work surface. Using the parchment paper, roll the cake up jelly roll–style starting at the narrow end of the cake. Set on a wire rack until cool, about 20 minutes.

5. *For the filling:* While the cake is cooling, using a hand mixer or a stand mixer fitted with the paddle attachment, beat the cream cheese, butter, vanilla, and powdered sugar until fluffy.

6. Carefully unroll the cake, spread the frosting evenly over the surface, and reroll the cake, removing the parchment as you roll. Wrap in plastic wrap and refrigerate for 1 hour.

7. *For the topping:* Mix together the powdered sugar and cinnamon. Sprinkle over the pumpkin roll, then slice and serve.

Cherry Fluff

Yield: Serves 12 | Prep Time: 15 minutes | Chill Time: 1 hour

This might be one of the easiest desserts you'll ever make. Simply combine all of the ingredients before dinner, throw it in the fridge, and forget about it until you're ready to serve it up. After the ruckus of holiday planning, you'll be grateful to have something this easy to rely on at the end.

INGREDIENTS

1 (20-ounce) can maraschino cherries, drained and halved

1 (20-ounce) can crushed pineapple, drained

1 (14-ounce) can sweetened condensed milk

1 (8-ounce) container whipped topping

2 cups mini marshmallows

1 cup sweetened shredded coconut

½ cup chopped pecans or walnuts, plus extra for serving

DIRECTIONS

Reserve some cherries for garnish. In a large bowl, combine the cherries, pineapple, condensed milk, and whipped topping. Fold in the mini marshmallows, shredded coconut, and pecans. Refrigerate for 1 hour. Spoon into parfait glasses, sprinkle with extra nuts and cherries, and serve.

Pumpkin Cheesecake Bars

Yield: Serves 10 to 12 | Prep Time: 20 minutes | Cook Time: 1 hour 50 minutes, plus 3 hours chill time

I love having these around during the holidays because they're more unique than the traditional pumpkin pie but still have that sweet autumn flavor. The addition of cream cheese makes these creamier and denser than traditional pumpkin pie.

INGREDIENTS

Crust

1½ cups graham cracker crumbs

4 tablespoons unsalted butter, melted

Filling

4 (8-ounce) packages cream cheese, room temperature

1½ cups sugar

4 large eggs

1 cup canned pumpkin puree

2 teaspoons pumpkin pie spice

Whipped topping

DIRECTIONS

1. *For the crust:* Preheat the oven to 300°F.

2. Line a 9 × 13-inch baking dish with parchment paper, leaving about 1 inch of paper hanging over the sides.

3. In a medium bowl, combine the graham cracker crumbs with the melted butter. With your fingers, press the crust into the bottom of the prepared pan. Set aside while making the filling.

4. *For the filling:* Using a hand mixer or a stand mixer fitted with the paddle attachment, beat the cream cheese and sugar on medium speed until light and fluffy. Beat in the eggs, one at a time, just until blended. Spoon half of the mixture over the crust and spread evenly.

5. Add the pumpkin puree and pumpkin pie spice to the remaining mixture. Beat until smooth. Carefully spoon over the mixture in the pan.

6. Bake for 50 minutes, or until just set. Turn off the oven and leave the door ajar, allowing the cheesecake to slowly cool down for about 1 hour or so. Refrigerate for at least 3 hours. Cut into bars, top with whipped topping, and serve.

Snickerdoodle Cobbler

Yield: Serves 8 | Prep Time: 10 minutes | Cook Time: 45 minutes

Cinnamon baking season starts as soon as I need to break out my fall jacket. I love mixing and matching ingredients to see what new recipes I can whip together using this fun autumn spice. This dessert takes the popular cookie flavor and turns it into a warm, fluffy cobbler.

INGREDIENTS

Cobbler

2 tablespoons unsalted butter

1 cup self-rising flour

¾ cup packed light brown sugar

1 teaspoon ground cinnamon

½ cup whole milk

1 teaspoon vanilla extract

Topping

¾ cup packed light brown sugar

1 teaspoon ground cinnamon

Caramel sauce

Whipped topping

DIRECTIONS

1. *For the cobbler:* Preheat the oven to 350°F.

2. Place the butter in an 8 × 8-inch glass baking dish and microwave for 30 seconds or until the butter has completely melted. Tilt the dish so the butter covers the entire bottom.

3. In a medium bowl, combine the flour, brown sugar, and cinnamon and toss lightly with a fork. Stir in the milk and vanilla until combined and all of the dry ingredients are incorporated. Spread the batter in the baking dish on top of the melted butter.

4. *For the topping:* In a small bowl, combine the brown sugar and cinnamon. Sprinkle the mixture on top of the batter.

5. Pour 1½ cups water into a microwave-safe bowl and microwave on high for 3 minutes, until the water boils. Pour the boiling water over the batter and topping to cover and moisten it all. Bake for 45 minutes. Let cool slightly. Drizzle with caramel sauce, top with whipped topping, and serve.

Mini Pecan Pies

Yield: Makes 24 mini pies | Prep Time: 15 minutes | Cook Time: 22 to 25 minutes

These bite-size pies are so adorable that even if everyone claims to be full, they can usually find room to sneak in one or two. Because they're easy to handle, you could even set them out on the hors d'oeuvres table during cocktail parties.

INGREDIENTS

⅓ cup unsalted butter, melted, plus butter for the muffin tin

Pie dough for 1 double-crust 9-inch pie (store-bought or homemade)

1 cup corn syrup

¾ cup granulated sugar

¼ cup packed light brown sugar

3 large eggs, beaten

¾ teaspoon vanilla extract

1 cup chopped pecans

DIRECTIONS

1. Preheat the oven to 350°F. Grease a 24-cup mini muffin tin with butter.

2. Roll out the pie dough and cut out 24 rounds with a 3-inch round cookie cutter. (I actually use a child's cup about 3 inches in diameter.) Press the pie crust rounds into the mini muffin tin.

3. In a medium bowl, whisk together the corn syrup, granulated sugar, brown sugar, eggs, vanilla, and melted butter. It will have the consistency of syrup.

4. Divide the pecans among the muffin cups. Pour about 2 tablespoons of pie filling on top of the pecans in each muffin cup. The pecans will float to the top.

5. Bake for 22 to 25 minutes until the crust is lightly browned. Let cool in the muffin tin for about 5 minutes. Remove the pies gently, using a fork if needed, and transfer to a wire rack. Let cool completely before serving.

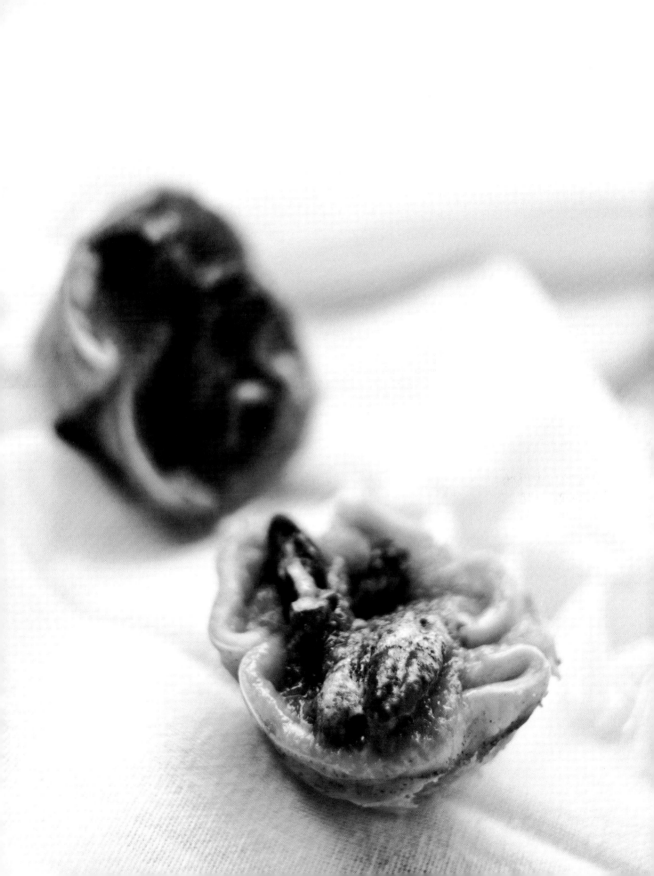

Slow Cooker Baked Apples

Yield: Serves 6 | Prep Time: 5 minutes | Cook Time: 2½ to 3 hours on high

If you're anything like me, you look for any excuse to indulge in dessert all day long. These baked apples make for a great breakfast the next morning. Top with a little Greek yogurt and oats, and you'll be happy there were leftovers.

INGREDIENTS

6 large Gala apples

¾ cup packed light brown sugar

¼ cup chopped walnuts or oats

2 tablespoons unsalted butter, softened and cut into pieces

1 teaspoon ground cinnamon

½ cup apple cider

Ice cream

Caramel sauce

DIRECTIONS

1. Wash and core the apples using a melon baller or paring knife, leaving about ½ inch on the bottom of the apple. Remove 1 inch from the top of the apples to prevent them from splitting.

2. In a medium bowl, combine the brown sugar, walnuts, butter, and cinnamon and fill each apple with the mixture. Place the apples in the slow cooker and pour the apple cider on top.

3. Cover and cook for 2½ to 3 hours on high, until the apples are soft when poked with a fork.

4. Serve with ice cream and caramel sauce.

Praline Bread Pudding with Caramel Sauce

Yield: Serves 10 | Prep Time: 1 hour 25 minutes | Cook Time: 55 minutes

Make sure to thoroughly dry out the bread cubes before baking. That makes it easier for them to soak up the custard, so each bite is as sweet as can be.

INGREDIENTS

Bread Pudding

1 (1-pound) loaf brioche or challah bread (see notes)

4 cups half-and-half

8 large eggs

1¼ cups packed light brown sugar

1 tablespoon vanilla extract

1 teaspoon ground cinnamon

Salted Caramel Sauce

½ cup packed light brown sugar

8 tablespoons unsalted butter, softened and cut into chunks

½ cup light corn syrup

1 tablespoon bourbon (optional)

1 tablespoon large flake sea salt

½ teaspoon vanilla extract

Topping

8 tablespoons unsalted butter, cold

½ cup packed light brown sugar

⅓ cup all-purpose flour

½ teaspoon salt

1½ cups coarsely chopped pecans

DIRECTIONS

1. *For the bread pudding:* Cut the brioche into 1-inch cubes and let dry on the counter overnight or toast lightly in a 200°F oven for 5 minutes.

2. Coat a deep 9 × 13-inch baking dish with cooking spray. Place the bread in the dish. In a large bowl, whisk the half-and-half and eggs until smooth. Add the brown sugar, vanilla, and cinnamon and stir to combine. Pour over the bread cubes, toss lightly to coat the bread, and let stand for 1 hour, gently stirring once or twice.

3. *For the salted caramel sauce:* In a small, heavy saucepan, combine the brown sugar, butter, and corn syrup and bring to a gentle boil over medium heat until the butter melts and the sugar dissolves. Immediately reduce to a low simmer and cook for 5 minutes, stirring only occasionally. Let cool for 5 minutes, then stir in the bourbon, if using, sea salt, and vanilla. Set aside to thicken.

4. *For the topping:* Preheat the oven to 350°F.

5. In a large bowl, combine the butter, brown sugar, flour, and salt with 2 forks or a pastry blender until you create large crumbles. Stir in the pecans and spread over the top of the bread mixture. Bake for 45 minutes. Let cool on a wire rack for at least 15 minutes. Gently reheat the caramel sauce, if necessary, drizzle over the bread pudding, and serve.

NOTES

This is best made with a sweet, eggy bread such as brioche or challah (like the Hanukkah Challah Bread on page 131). If unavailable, use Hawaiian bread or a similar bread if possible.

The caramel sauce needs to be made slightly ahead to cool and thicken, and can be made hours ahead of time, covered and refrigerated, and gently reheated. The recipe makes 1½ cups of sauce. Refrigerate any leftover sauce to drizzle over ice cream or other desserts.

Peppermint Crunch Balls

Yield: Makes 24 cookies | Prep Time: 15 minutes, plus 1 hour chill time | Cook Time: 10 to 12 minutes

Peppermint is one of the top flavors of the Christmas season. These quick-cooking holiday balls are an excellent, festive addition to your annual cookie exchange.

INGREDIENTS

1 cup (2 sticks) unsalted butter, softened

1 cup powdered sugar

1 large egg

½ teaspoon vanilla extract

½ teaspoon peppermint extract

¼ teaspoon salt

3 drops red food coloring

2½ cups all-purpose flour

1 cup finely crushed peppermint candies (such as Starlight mints)

3 tablespoons turbinado sugar

DIRECTIONS

1. Using a stand mixer with the paddle attachment, beat the butter and powdered sugar on medium speed until light and fluffy. Add the egg, vanilla and peppermint extracts, salt, and red food coloring; beat until well blended. Gradually add the flour and beat until thoroughly blended. Cover the bowl with plastic wrap and refrigerate for 1 hour.

2. Preheat the oven to 375°F. Coat 2 baking sheets with cooking spray.

3. In a small bowl, combine the crushed peppermint candies and turbinado sugar. Shape the chilled cookie dough into 1-inch balls and roll each ball in the candy cane mixture. Place 2 inches apart on the baking sheets. The cookies will spread slightly.

4. Bake for 10 to 12 minutes, or until golden. Immediately remove to wire racks to cool completely. Serve.

Homemade Holiday Reindeer Poop

Yield: Makes 24 cookies | Prep Time: 1 hour | Cook Time: n/a

If you're going to any event where kids will be around, I can guarantee this recipe will be a hit. Make sure to label them as "Reindeer Poop," so everyone's in on the joke!

INGREDIENTS

4 tablespoons unsalted butter

1 (5-ounce) bag mini marshmallows

¼ teaspoon salt

1 (12-ounce) jar caramel ice cream topping

12 ounces semisweet chocolate chips

4 cups crispy rice cereal

1 cup M&M'S candies

DIRECTIONS

1. In a 3-quart saucepan, melt the butter over medium-low heat. Add the mini marshmallows and salt and stir until completely melted and well combined.

2. Remove the saucepan from the heat. Add the caramel sauce, stirring until the mixture is smooth. Add the chocolate chips and continue stirring until the chocolate has melted. Mix in the crispy rice cereal, being sure everything is well coated. Add the M&M'S and mix until evenly distributed.

3. Spray your hands lightly with cooking spray and carefully scoop small piles of the mixture onto parchment paper. Let them cool for about 15 minutes before serving. The cookies will continue to harden as they continue cooling. Store in an airtight container in a cool place for up to a week.

Peanut Butter Snowballs

Yield: Makes 20 snowballs | Prep Time: 15 minutes | Chill Time: 1 hour 50 minutes

Create your own winter wonderland with these irresistible Peanut Butter Snowballs. Bundle these up in decorative baggies to give away as gifts or put them in a fun bowl to leave out during a holiday party.

INGREDIENTS

1 cup powdered sugar

½ cup creamy peanut butter

4 tablespoons unsalted butter, softened

¼ teaspoon vanilla extract

¼ teaspoon salt

1 pound white chocolate morsels

DIRECTIONS

1. Line a baking sheet with parchment paper. In a medium bowl, combine the powdered sugar, peanut butter, butter, vanilla, and salt. Refrigerate until the dough is firm, about 1 hour. Shape the dough into 1-inch balls and place on the prepared baking sheet. Freeze the balls for about 30 minutes.

2. Melt the white chocolate candy coating according to the directions on the package. Dip the balls in the chocolate mixture. Return them to the baking sheet and refrigerate until the coating is set, about 20 minutes, before serving.

Red Velvet Cheesecake Brownies

Yield: Makes 12 squares | Prep Time: 10 minutes | Cook Time: 30 minutes

This beautiful marbled dessert gives you the best of both worlds: the creaminess of a freshly baked cheesecake mixed with the decadent chocolate taste of brownies.

INGREDIENTS

Bars

1 cup sugar

8 tablespoons unsalted butter, melted

¼ cup unsweetened cocoa powder

1 tablespoon red food coloring

1 teaspoon instant espresso powder

½ teaspoon vanilla extract

⅛ teaspoon salt

½ teaspoon white vinegar

2 large eggs

¾ cup all-purpose flour

Cheesecake Filling

1 (8-ounce) package cream cheese, softened

3 tablespoons sugar

1 large egg yolk

½ teaspoon vanilla extract

DIRECTIONS

1. *For the bars:* Preheat the oven to 350°F. Line an 8 × 8-inch baking dish with parchment paper. Lightly coat the parchment paper with cooking spray and set aside.

2. In a large bowl, stir the sugar, melted butter, cocoa powder, food coloring, espresso powder, vanilla, and salt until completely combined. Stir in the vinegar.

3. In a small bowl, whisk the eggs together. Pour the eggs into the large bowl and mix to combine. Slowly add the flour, stirring after each addition until just combined. Pour the batter into the baking dish and set aside.

4. *For the cheesecake filling:* Using a hand mixer or a stand mixer fitted with the paddle attachment, beat the cream cheese, sugar, egg yolk, and vanilla until well combined. Spread the cream cheese mixture in an even layer over the brownie batter. Using a knife, swirl the cream cheese together with the brownie batter.

5. Bake the brownies for 30 minutes. Remove them from the oven and let cool completely before lifting the parchment out of the pan. Slice into squares and serve.

Old-Fashioned Homemade Fudge

Yield: Makes 25 squares | Prep Time: 5 minutes | Chill Time: 1 hour

Old-fashioned holiday fudge is such a fun and unexpected gift to make for friends—and this one uses just three ingredients. I like to present it in decorative boxes from the local craft store to really spruce things up.

INGREDIENTS

18 ounces semisweet chocolate chips

1 (14-ounce) can sweetened condensed milk

4 tablespoons unsalted butter, softened

DIRECTIONS

1. Coat an 8 × 8-inch baking dish very generously with cooking spray. Set aside.

2. In a large microwave-safe bowl, combine the chocolate chips, sweetened condensed milk, and butter. Microwave, removing the mixture from the microwave and stirring every 30 seconds, until the chocolate is completely melted.

3. Pour the mixture into the baking dish. Smooth with a spatula and refrigerate for 1 hour, or until set. Remove the fudge from the dish and cut into squares. Serve.

Gingerbread People

Yield: Makes 24 gingerbread people | Prep Time: 15 to 20 minutes | Cook Time: 8 to 10 minutes

My aunt used to love making these, and around the holiday season, her kitchen was so inviting because it smelled like so many different spices. I remember her spending so much time decorating them and hanging each off the banister, tucked so perfectly into the garland. That was, until my uncle would slowly bite off their limbs as he walked up and down the stairs. At first she didn't notice, but slowly they would lose a head or arm, and of course we kids thought it was the funniest thing ever.

INGREDIENTS

3 cups all-purpose flour, plus extra for the work surface

½ teaspoon kosher salt

1 tablespoon ground ginger

2 teaspoons ground cinnamon

½ teaspoon ground allspice

¼ teaspoon ground cloves

6 tablespoons unsalted butter, softened

¾ cup packed dark brown sugar

1 large egg

½ cup molasses

2 teaspoons vanilla extract

1 teaspoon grated orange zest

DIRECTIONS

1. Preheat the oven to 375°F. Line a baking sheet with parchment paper.

2. In a medium bowl, whisk together the flour, salt, ginger, cinnamon, allspice, and cloves. Set aside.

3. Using a stand mixer fitted with the paddle attachment, beat the butter and brown sugar together on medium speed until creamy. Add the egg and beat well. Add the molasses, vanilla, and orange zest and beat until combined. Reduce the speed to low and add the flour mixture slowly, mixing until a dough is formed.

4. Divide the dough in half. Refrigerate 1 half while you roll the other half on a lightly floured surface to ¼ inch thick. Use a cookie cutter to cut out gingerbread people, transfer them to the prepared baking sheet, and bake for 8 to 10 minutes.

5. Let cool on the baking sheet for a few minutes, then carefully place the cookies on a wire rack to cool further. Repeat with the remaining dough. Decorate and serve.

Sparkling Cranberry Cake

Yield: Serves 8 to 10 | Prep Time: 30 minutes, plus chill overnight | Cook Time: 40 minutes

This may be my all-time favorite cake because the glittered cranberries sparkle like the twinkle in Santa's eye.

INGREDIENTS

Cranberries

1½ cups sugar

1 cup water

2 cups fresh cranberries

Cake

3⅓ cups all-purpose flour

2 cups sugar

2½ teaspoons baking powder

1½ cups (3 sticks) unsalted butter, softened

1 cup sour cream

1 cup whole milk

3 large eggs

2 tablespoons vanilla extract

3 cups fresh cranberries

Frosting

12 ounces white chocolate morsels

¾ cup heavy cream

¾ cup unsalted butter, softened

9 cups powdered sugar

DIRECTIONS

1. *For the cranberries:* Combine 1 cup sugar and the water in a large saucepan and simmer over medium heat until the sugar has completely dissolved. Pour the simple syrup into a bowl and let cool for about 10 minutes. Stir in the cranberries. Cover and refrigerate overnight.

2. Remove the cranberries and roll in the remaining ½ cup sugar. Set the cranberries aside to dry for about 30 minutes.

3. *For the cake:* Preheat the oven to 350°F. Coat three 8-inch cake pans with cooking spray and place parchment paper in the bottom of the pans.

4. In a large bowl, whisk together the flour, sugar, and baking powder. Add the butter, sour cream, milk, eggs, and vanilla just until smooth. Stir in the cranberries. Divide the batter evenly between the 3 cake pans.

5. Bake for 35 to 40 minutes, until a toothpick inserted comes out clean. Let cool for 10 minutes, then invert onto a wire rack to cool completely.

6. *For the frosting:* Place the white chocolate chips in a large bowl.

7. Microwave the cream until it starts to boil. Pour over the chips. Cover the bowl with plastic wrap and let sit for about 5 minutes, then whisk until smooth. Let sit until thick.

8. Using a hand mixer, beat the frosting until smooth. Beat in the butter. Slowly add the powdered sugar and beat until light and fluffy.

9. *To assemble the cake:* Place a cake layer on a cake plate. Spread some frosting over the cake in an even layer. Repeat with the next 2 layers, frosting the top and sides of the cake. Top with sparkling cranberries and add some around the edge, if desired. Slice and serve.

No-Bake Holiday Fruitcake

Yield: Serves 9 | Prep Time: 5 minutes | Chill Time: 8 hours

Fruitcakes have been a Christmas staple for decades. They're colorful, festive, and keep quite well. This no-bake version is great because you can still have a fabulous dessert even if the oven is stuffed full of cookies, appetizers, and side dishes.

INGREDIENTS

1 (13.5-ounce) package graham crackers, crushed

2 (6-ounce) containers dried and sweetened cherries

1 (6-ounce) container candied pineapple, chopped

2 (14-ounce) cans sweetened condensed milk

1½ cups coarsely chopped pecans

DIRECTIONS

1. Line an 8 × 8-inch baking dish with plastic wrap, letting the plastic wrap hang over the sides a few inches.

2. In a large bowl, combine the crushed graham crackers, cherries, pineapple, condensed milk, and pecans and thoroughly mix with your clean hands. Transfer the mixture to the prepared baking dish, press into an even layer, and cover well. Freeze for at least 8 hours, or overnight.

3. To serve, remove from the freezer, invert onto a serving platter, remove the dish and plastic wrap, and cut into squares.

Lemon Crinkle Cookies

Yield: Makes 24 cookies | Prep Time: 30 minutes, plus 1 hour chill time | Cook Time: 10 to 12 minutes

The holidays are usually bogged down with such heavy foods that it's nice to serve something lighter to brighten up the day. These cookies remind me of the sunshine bursting through a cloudy, gloomy winter day and always make me smile.

INGREDIENTS

8 tablespoons unsalted butter, softened

1 cup granulated sugar

1 large egg

1 teaspoon very finely grated lemon zest plus 1½ tablespoons lemon juice

½ teaspoon vanilla extract

1½ cups all-purpose flour

¼ teaspoon salt

¼ teaspoon baking powder

⅛ teaspoon baking soda

½ cup powdered sugar

DIRECTIONS

1. Preheat the oven to 350°F. Line a baking sheet with parchment paper.

2. Using a hand mixer, beat the butter and granulated sugar in a large bowl on medium speed until smooth. Add the egg, lemon juice, and vanilla. Beat in the flour, salt, baking powder, and baking soda on low speed. Refrigerate for 1 hour, or until firm.

3. In a small bowl, combine the powdered sugar and lemon zest.

4. Working with about a tablespoon of dough at a time, roll the dough into 1-inch balls between your palms. Roll each ball in the powdered sugar mixture until well coated. Place them 2 inches apart on the baking sheet and bake for 10 to 12 minutes, until crinkly on top and light brown on the bottom. Let cool for 5 minutes before serving.

Christmas Magic Squares

Yield: Makes 18 bars | Prep Time: 10 minutes | Cook Time: 30 minutes

Magic squares are always the hit of the night anytime they're brought out. They're so gooey and sweet that they're difficult to resist. If you want to make these at other times of the year, just swap out the red and green M&M'S for multicolored ones and replace the mint chocolate–covered candies with butterscotch chips.

INGREDIENTS

8 tablespoons unsalted butter

1½ cups graham cracker crumbs

12 ounces semisweet chocolate chips

1 cup chopped pecans

1 cup sweetened flaked coconut

1 (14-ounce) can sweetened condensed milk

½ cup mint chocolate–covered candies

½ cup red and green M&M'S

DIRECTIONS

1. Preheat the oven to 350°F. Put the butter in a 9 × 13-inch baking dish, then place in the oven for 5 minutes, or until the butter has melted.

2. Layer the graham cracker crumbs, chocolate chips, pecans, and coconut over the butter. Pour the sweetened condensed milk over the coconut; top with the mint chocolate–covered candies and red and green M&M'S.

3. Bake for 30 minutes. Set the baking dish on a wire rack and let cool completely. Cut into squares and serve.

Homemade Cracker Candy

Yield: Serves 8 to 10 | Prep Time: 10 minutes | Cook Time: 5 minutes, plus 1½ hours chill time

Holiday candy makes for a great gift to bundle up nice and pretty and hand out to everyone you see on a regular basis: the postal worker, your coworkers, you name it! It's a nice way of showing you care and spreading holiday cheer.

INGREDIENTS

24 round buttery crackers

12 tablespoons unsalted butter

¾ cup packed light brown sugar

Pinch salt

½ teaspoon vanilla extract

12 ounces semisweet chocolate chips

½ cup chopped pecans

8 ounces white chocolate morsels, melted

DIRECTIONS

1. Preheat the oven to 350°F. Line a 9 × 13-inch baking sheet with parchment paper and lightly coat with cooking spray.

2. Arrange the crackers in a single layer in the pan.

3. In a small saucepan, combine the butter, brown sugar, and salt and bring to a boil over medium heat. Boil gently for 3 minutes, stirring constantly. Remove from the heat and stir in the vanilla. Pour the mixture over the crackers.

4. Bake for 5 minutes and remove from the oven. Sprinkle the top with the chocolate chips and return to the oven until the chocolate has melted. Remove from the oven again, and sprinkle the pecans over the chocolate. Drizzle with the melted white chocolate.

5. Refrigerate 1½ hours or until firm. Break into pieces and serve.

NOTES

The cracker candy can be stored in an airtight container in the refrigerator for up to a week.

Hanukkah Gelt

Yield: Makes 48 coins | Prep Time: 10 minutes | Cook Time: n/a

Chocolate gelt, or chocolate coins, are typically given to children during Hanukkah. While you can find these in stores, it's fun to make your own and paint them with edible gold dust.

INGREDIENTS

8 ounces dark chocolate morsels

Edible gold luster dust

DIRECTIONS

1. Put the chocolate in a glass bowl and microwave for 30 seconds. Remove the bowl, stir the chocolate, and repeat until the chocolate is completely melted and smooth. Have ready two 24-cup mini muffin tins.

2. Drop a small amount of chocolate into the bottom of each muffin cup. There should be enough to cover the bottom of each muffin cup and up the sides about ⅛ of an inch. Tap the muffin tins on the counter a few times to release any bubbles and to smooth the tops of the chocolate. Freeze for 10 minutes.

3. Turn the muffin tins upside down and tap on the counter. The coins will release easily. Using a small clean paintbrush, brush each coin with the gold dust. Serve.

NOTES

To store, place in a plastic zip-top bag in the refrigerator for up to 1 week.

Hanukkah Jelly Donuts

Yield: Makes 20 donuts | Prep Time: 45 minutes to 1 hour, plus 1½ hours proof time | Cook Time: 80 seconds for every 2 donuts

Fried foods are a staple during Hanukkah as an homage to the miracle of the holiday, when one day's worth of oil lasted for eight days. This dish pays tribute in the tastiest way I know!

INGREDIENTS

¾ cup whole milk, warmed to 110°F

¼ cup plus 1 teaspoon granulated sugar

2 tablespoons active dry yeast

2¼ cups all-purpose flour, plus extra for the work surface

3 egg yolks

2 tablespoons unsalted butter, softened

1 teaspoon kosher salt

3 cups vegetable oil, plus extra for the bowl

Granulated sugar or powdered sugar

1 cup raspberry or strawberry jam

DIRECTIONS

1. In a small bowl, combine the milk, 1 teaspoon of the granulated sugar, and the yeast. Let stand until the mixture is foamy, 5 to 10 minutes.

2. Put the flour in a large bowl and make a well in the center. Add the egg yolks, butter, salt, yeast mixture, and remaining ¼ cup granulated sugar. Using a wooden spoon, stir the mixture until a sticky dough forms.

3. Turn the dough onto a lightly floured work surface and knead for 8 to 10 minutes, until smooth and elastic. Form the dough into a ball and place in a lightly oiled bowl. Cover with plastic wrap and set in a warm place to rise until the dough has doubled in size, about 1½ hours.

4. Roll the dough out on a lightly floured work surface to ¼-inch thick. Using a 2½-inch round cutter, cut 20 rounds of dough. Cover with plastic wrap and let rise for 15 minutes. Line a baking sheet with paper towels.

5. In a deep skillet, heat the vegetable oil over medium heat until the temperature reaches 370°F.

6. Carefully place 2 rounds in the oil and fry for about 40 seconds. Turn the donuts over and fry for an additional 40 seconds, until golden. Remove with a slotted spoon and place on the baking sheet. One at a time, roll in granulated sugar or sprinkle with powdered sugar while still warm.

7. Fit a pastry bag with a #4 pastry tip and fill the bag with the jam. Using a wooden skewer, make a hole in the side of each donut. Fit the pastry tip into the hole and pipe about 2 teaspoons of jam into the donut; repeat to fill all the donuts. Serve.

Rugelach

Yield: Makes 48 cookies | Prep Time: 30 minutes, plus 2 hours 20 minutes chill time | Cook Time: 20 to 22 minutes

Rugelach is a Jewish pastry that I love for its versatility. I used raspberry preserves for the center to give these cookies a festive spin, but you have so many different options, from chocolate-hazelnut spread to cream cheese to cinnamon-sugar and more!

INGREDIENTS

2 cups all-purpose flour

1 cup (2 sticks) unsalted butter, cold, diced

1 (8-ounce) package cream cheese, cold, chopped

⅓ cup sour cream

2 tablespoons sugar, plus extra for the work surface

¼ teaspoon salt

1 (12-ounce) jar all-fruit raspberry preserves

1 cup sliced almonds

DIRECTIONS

1. In a food processor, pulse the flour, butter, cream cheese, sour cream, sugar, and salt until the mixture is crumbly. Turn the mixture out onto a work surface and shape into 4 equal disks. Wrap each disk in plastic wrap and refrigerate for 2 hours or up to 2 days.

2. Sprinkle a work surface with sugar and then roll 1 disk into a 9-inch round, keeping the remaining disks chilled until ready to use. Spread a thin layer of raspberry preserves on the round and then sprinkle with one-quarter of the almonds. With a pizza cutter or large sharp knife, cut the round into 12 wedges. Roll the wedges from the widest edge to the narrowest. Repeat with the remaining dough, jam, and almonds.

3. Place the rugelach on ungreased baking sheets and refrigerate for at least 20 minutes. Preheat the oven to 350°F.

4. Bake for 20 to 22 minutes until lightly golden. Let cool completely on wire racks before serving.

NOTES

Store in an airtight container for up to 1 week or freeze for later.

Happy New Year Fortune Cookies

Yield: Makes 18 to 20 cookies | Prep Time: 15 minutes | Cook Time: 30 minutes

These make for a wonderful party favor anytime. I love to customize fortunes for my guests to give them best wishes and hopeful messages for the new year.

INGREDIENTS

3 egg whites

¾ cup sugar

8 tablespoons unsalted butter, melted and cooled

¼ teaspoon vanilla extract

¼ teaspoon almond extract

3 tablespoons water

1 cup all-purpose flour

Fortune cookie strips

DIRECTIONS

1. Preheat the oven to 375°F. Line a baking sheet with a silicone pad or parchment paper.

2. Using a hand mixer, whip the egg whites and sugar in a large bowl on medium speed until the mixture is frothy. Add the melted butter and mix until combined. Add the vanilla and almond extracts and water and mix until combined. Beat in the flour until combined.

3. Using a tablespoon, spoon the batter onto the baking sheet in 3 places, and spread each into a 3-inch circle. (Only bake 3 cookies at a time. They set up very quickly, and you need time to form the fortune cookies.) Bake the cookies for 8 minutes, until the edges are lightly browned. (Do not overbake, or they will be too brittle to form.)

4. Remove the baking sheet from the oven and loosen each cookie from the baking sheet by running a small spatula underneath. Place the fortune in the center of each cookie and fold over into a semicircle.

5. Quickly place 1 cookie over the edge of a mug and press down to shape into a fortune cookie shape, pressing the edges together and bending in the middle. Place the cookie in the cup of a muffin tin to help hold the shape until it has cooled and the shape has set. Repeat with the remaining cookies. Serve.

NOTES

You can find fortune cookie text on the internet, or you can make your own.

Champagne and Strawberry Cake Balls

Yield: Makes about 32 cake balls | Prep Time: 5 minutes | Cook Time: 30 to 35 minutes, plus 3 hours chill time

Is there any better New Year's Eve combination than cake mix and champagne? These cute pink treats are a fun and decorative addition to your party spread.

INGREDIENTS

1 (15.2-ounce) box strawberry cake mix

1¼ cups champagne

⅓ cup vegetable oil

3 large eggs

1 (16-ounce) container white cake frosting

1½ pounds white chocolate morsels

DIRECTIONS

1. Preheat the oven to 350°F. Lightly coat a 9 × 13-inch baking dish with cooking spray.

2. In a large bowl, combine the cake mix, champagne, oil, and eggs until smooth. Pour the batter into the baking dish. Bake for 30 to 35 minutes, until a toothpick inserted in the center comes out clean. Let the cake cool completely.

3. Crumble the cake into a large bowl. Add the frosting to the cake crumbs and mix until evenly combined. Refrigerate for at least 2 hours to firm up.

4. Line a baking sheet with parchment paper. Form small round balls by rolling a rounded tablespoon's worth of mixture between your palms and place on the baking sheet. Place the baking sheet in the freezer for 1 hour.

5. Place the white chocolate in a microwave-safe bowl and microwave until melted and smooth, stirring at 30-second intervals. Remove the balls from the freezer and lightly drizzle with the melted chocolate. Return the balls to the baking tray to allow the chocolate to harden. Serve.

6

Drinks

Bottoms up! The holidays get a little bit cheerier when a
signature holiday drink makes an appearance. From homemade
versions of classics like eggnog to New Year's specialties
like champagne cocktails, there's plenty here to love.

Slow Cooker Mulled Cider

Yield: Serves 6 to 8 | Prep Time: 5 minutes | Cook Time: 1 hour on high or 2 hours on low

The holidays are full of cinnamon, spice, and everything nice, including plenty of mulled cider to go around. I love making a batch on the weekends around the holidays, so my husband and I can snuggle up with a piping hot mug, a blanket, our puppy, and one of our favorite holiday movies.

INGREDIENTS

1 gallon apple cider

½ cup packed light brown sugar

2 teaspoons allspice berries

3 teaspoons whole cloves

4 sticks cinnamon

2 dashes grated nutmeg

1 orange, unpeeled, thinly sliced

1 cup cranberries

1 apple, peeled, cored, and sliced into matchsticks

DIRECTIONS

1. Pour the cider into a 6-quart slow cooker. Stir in the brown sugar.

2. Place the allspice, cloves, cinnamon, and nutmeg in a small piece of cheesecloth. Carefully fold up the cloth, making sure none of the spices can fall out. Tie up with kitchen twine and place in the slow cooker. Add the orange slices, cranberries, and apple pieces. Cover and cook for 1 hour on high or for 2 hours on low. Ladle into glasses and serve.

VARIATIONS

This recipe can be made on the stovetop in a large pot. Cover and let slowly simmer for 30 minutes.

Salted Caramel Eggnog

Yield: Serves 6 | Prep Time: 5 minutes | Cook Time: 10 minutes

In my house, the Christmas season isn't officially here until I've had my first sip of eggnog. The creamy, thick, eggy texture is like the liquid version of a hug. The salted caramel adds a gourmet touch that's like something you'd get from a fancy café.

INGREDIENTS

3 cups whole milk

1 cup heavy cream

4 cinnamon sticks

2¼ teaspoons vanilla extract

1 teaspoon grated nutmeg, plus extra for garnish

5 large eggs

⅔ cup sugar

¾ cup dark rum

½ cup caramel syrup

1 tablespoon sea salt

Whipped topping

DIRECTIONS

1. In a large saucepan, combine the milk, cream, cinnamon, vanilla, and nutmeg. Bring to a boil over medium heat. Be careful that the milk doesn't boil over the pan. As soon as you see it bubbling, remove from the heat. Let sit for 5 to 10 minutes to steep.

2. Using a stand mixer fitted with the paddle attachment, beat the eggs and sugar on medium-high speed until fully combined. Pour the egg mixture into the milk and whisk quickly until fully combined. Add the rum, caramel syrup, and salt and whisk to combine.

3. Pour the eggnog into 6 glasses, leaving a bit of room at the top. Garnish with whipped topping and nutmeg and serve.

Slow Cooker Peppermint Hot Chocolate

Yield: Serves 8 to 10 | Prep Time: 5 minutes | Cook Time: 2 hours on Low

When I come back inside after a day of ice skating and romping around in the snow, I love to have something warm and cozy waiting to thaw me out. All I have to do is prep this peppermint hot chocolate ahead of time, turn it on, and know it'll be waiting for me after my wintry day of fun.

INGREDIENTS

5 ½ cups whole milk

2 cups heavy cream

1 (14-ounce) can sweetened condensed milk

12 ounces milk chocolate chips

1 teaspoon peppermint extract

Frozen whipped topping

Crushed candy canes

DIRECTIONS

Combine the milk, cream, condensed milk, chocolate chips, and peppermint extract in a 6-quart slow cooker. Cover and cook on Low for 2 hours, stirring occasionally. Pour into mugs and top with whipped topping and crushed candy canes. Serve.

Champagne Cranberry Cocktail

Yield: Serves 3 | Prep Time: 5 minutes | Cook Time: n/a

Break out the champagne! The holidays are a time for celebration and merriment, and this cranberry-infused champagne concoction adds a bubbly pop to the day.

INGREDIENTS

1 cup cranberries, plus extra for garnish

1 cup sugar

1 (26-ounce) bottle champagne

DIRECTIONS

1. In a medium saucepan, combine the cranberries, sugar, and 1 cup water. Bring to a boil and simmer until the sugar is dissolved and the mixture is syrupy. Strain the mixture through a sieve into a bowl, discarding the cranberries.

2. Pour 8 ounces of the champagne into each glass. Add 1 ounce cranberry simple syrup to each glass. Garnish with extra cranberries and serve.

Lemon Rosé Cocktail

Yield: Serves 1 | Prep Time: 5 minutes | Cook Time: n/a

This cocktail is one of my secret dinner party tricks. By adding just a couple of sweet touches to a dry rosé wine, you can create something elegant and unique that'll take your entertaining to the next level.

INGREDIENTS

1 cup sugar

2 tablespoons lemon juice

6 ounces dry rosé wine

Candied lemon peel for garnish

DIRECTIONS

1. In a medium saucepan, combine the sugar, 1 cup water, and the lemon juice. Bring to a boil and simmer until the sugar is dissolved and the mixture is syrupy. Strain the mixture through a sieve into a bowl.

2. Pour 6 ounces rosé wine into a glass. Add 1 ounce lemon simple syrup. Garnish with candied lemon.

Acknowledgments

It was not long after I began dating Alex that I met his extended family. I was instantly welcomed into their world and their Christmas celebrations. For me, Christmas is the most magical time of year, and when family and friends are surrounding the fire, the table is glistening with dinner and drinks, and stockings are hung waiting for cheer, any sadness or sorrow is temporarily forgotten. Spending the holidays with Alex's family has taught me about the magic of this season. Every aunt, uncle, cousin, sibling, and pet has become a very special part of my holiday experience, and I can no longer imagine spending these special times without these incredible people. Thank you to all of them for showing me the true meaning and spirit of the holidays.

Thank you to my incredible culinary and creative team at Prime Publishing. Megan Von Schönhoff, my photographer. Chris Hammond, Judith Hines, and Marlene Stolfo, my culinary test kitchen geniuses. To Brant Janeway, Erica Martirano, Jaclyn Waggner, and Justine Sha, for helping to get these books out into the world and into the hands of home cooks everywhere. Thank you to Stuart Hochwert and the entire team at Prime Publishing for their support. To word masters and editors Bryn Clark and Jessica Thelander. And to my amazing editor and friend, Kara Rota. This book was a team effort, filled with collaboration and creativity that reached no limits.

Index

About the Author

After receiving her masters in culinary arts at Auguste Escoffier in Avignon, France, Addie stayed in France to learn from Christian Etienne at his three Michelin-star restaurant. Upon leaving France, she spent the next several years working with restaurant groups. She worked in the kitchen for Daniel Boulud and moved coast to coast with Thomas Keller building a career in management, restaurant openings, and brand development. She later joined Martha Stewart Living Omnimedia, where she worked with the editorial team as well as in marketing and sales. While living in New York, Addie completed her bachelor's degree in organizational behavior. Upon leaving New York, Addie joined gravitytank, an innovation consultancy in Chicago. As a culinary designer at gravitytank, Addie designed new food products for companies, large and small. She created edible prototypes for clients and research participants to taste and experience, some of which you may see in stores today. In 2015, she debuted on The Food Network, where she competed on *Cutthroat Kitchen*, and won. And in 2017, she was a contestant on *Food Network Star*.

Addie is the executive producer for RecipeLion. Addie oversees and creates culinary content for multiple web platforms and communities, leads video strategy, and oversees the production of in-print books. Addie is passionate about taking easy recipes and making them elegant, without making them complicated. From fine dining to entertaining, to innovation and test kitchens, Addie's experience with food makes these recipes unique and delicious.

Addie and her husband, Alex, live in Lake Forest, Illinois, with their baby boy and happy puppy, Paisley. Addie is actively involved with youth culinary programs in the Chicagoland area, serving on the board of a bakery and catering company that employs at-risk youth. She is a healthy-food teacher for first-graders in a low-income school district and, aside from eating and entertaining with friends and family, she loves encouraging kids to be creative in the kitchen!